KU-165-506

# THE
# SIX
# NATIONS
# RUGBY
## MISCELLANY

### SECOND EDITION

I am dedicating this book to my two sons, Marc and Paul.

Boys, I love you both.

Forever yours,

Dad

First edition published in 2009
Second edition published in 2013

Copyright © Carlton Books Limited 2009, 2013

Carlton Books Limited
20 Mortimer Street
London W1T 3JW

All rights reserved. No part of this publication may be reproduced, stored
in a retrieval system, or transmitted in any form or by any means, electronic,
mechanical, photocopying, recording or otherwise, without the prior
permission of the copyright owner and the publishers.

A CIP catalogue record for this book is available from the British Library

ISBN: 978-1-78097-377-7

Commissioning Editor: Martin Corteel
Editorial Assistant: David Ballheimer
Project Art Editor: Darren Jordan
Production: Maria Petalidou

Printed and bound by CPI Group (UK) Ltd, Croydon, CR0 4YY

# THE
# SIX
# NATIONS
# RUGBY
## MISCELLANY

### SECOND EDITION

## JOHN WHITE

WITH A FOREWORD BY **WILLIE JOHN McBRIDE,** MBE

CARLTON
BOOKS

# ❧ FOREWORD ❧

I was absolutely delighted when John, a fellow Irishman, approached me and asked me to write the foreword to this his *Six Nations Rugby Miscellany*. And thanks to Carlton Publishing for making a donation to the Wooden Spoon Society, which is very close to my heart.

Although I played rugby at school in Northern Ireland for the Ballymena Academy XV, it wasn't until my late teens before I began to play the game regularly. When I left school, I signed for my local club, Ballymena RC. I played lock and must have been doing something right because I will never forget the feeling of shock, quickly followed by an emotional high, when I was called up to the Irish national side. I was as proud as any Irish man before me when I pulled on the famous green jersey for the first time, winning my first cap against England at Twickenham on 10 February 1962. We lost 16–0 that day but the memory will last with me for ever. Although my Dad passed away when I was just four years old, I just knew he had a huge smile on his face as he looked down on me. If winning my first cap for Ireland was a huge surprise, then can you imagine how I felt when I was told I was included in the British Lions squad to tour South Africa in 1962? We lost that Test series 3–0 (with one draw) to the Springboks side but we learned a lot from the experience, which helped us immensely in our future tours. On 10 April 1965, I was a member of the Irish side that defeated South Africa for the first time, a 9–6 win at Lansdowne Road, and then we went one better at the Sydney Cricket Ground on 10 May 1967 when we became the first Five Nations side to beat Australia in their own back yard, an 11–5 win. It was also the first time a Home Nations side had defeated a major southern hemisphere team in their own country.

I toured with the Lions again in 1966 to Canada, Australia and New Zealand (lost 4–0) and again when we lost 3–0 to South Africa in 1968. In 1971, I went on my fourth Lions tour to face the mighty All Blacks. New Zealand was without question the greatest team in the world at the time, almost invincible, and many sports writers thought we would come home well beaten. However, every one of our squad played their part in what was a historic 2–1 (with a draw) Test series victory, the Lions' first and last Test series win over the All Blacks. My fifth and final Lions tour came in 1974, captaining the side to our first ever Test series win over South Africa (3–0 with one draw). On 15 March 1975, I called time on my international career, pulling on the Irish jersey for the 63rd and final time in a 32–4 loss to Wales at Cardiff Arms Park. In all, I captained Ireland 11 times and won a record 17 Test caps for the British Lions, not bad for a boy from Moneyglass, County Antrim.

**Willie John McBride, MBE**

## ❧ ACKNOWLEDGEMENTS ❧

I would like to take this opportunity to thank a number of people for helping me with my book.

Firstly, my wife Janice for painstakingly proofreading my work, the 11th time she has done this in my *Miscellany* range of books for Carlton Publishing.

Secondly, to my two sons, Marc and Paul: thanks, boys, for your helpful suggestions, particularly on the Irish players.

Thirdly, a word of thanks to Big Mike Hartley and Bill Clarkson for their valued input.

Fourthly, a great deal of thanks must go to Kevin Lassen, my All Blacks mate, who assisted me with many of the tables that can be found in the book. Kevin's website, http://www.pickandgo.info/, is a magnificent tool for finding out just about all you ever wanted to know about Rugby Union on the internet.

Finally, a special mention must go to Martin Corteel and his dedicated team at Carlton Publishing, who are just an absolute joy to work with as nothing is too much trouble for them.

And in closing, as the legendary lead singer of one of my favourite bands, the incomparable Freddie Mercury of Queen, once sang: *I Thank You One and All*.

John

# ❧ INTRODUCTION ❧

*"Now this is the Law of the Jungle – as old and as true as the sky;*
*And the Wolf that shall keep it may prosper, but the Wolf that shall break it must die.*
*As the creeper that girdles the tree-trunk the Law runneth forward and back –*
*For the strength of the Pack is the Wolf, and the strength of the Wolf is the Pack."*

The above lines from the famous Rudyard Kipling poem "The Law of the Jungle" in many ways epitomize Rugby Union for me. Rugby has a strict set of laws; the team committing the most offences in a game invariably ends up the losers; the forwards are supported by a back row as true as the strength of a 300-year-old oak tree, while a winger may break free from the pack and claim glory for that pack. On our television screens week in and week out we see sportsmen proudly taking to fields of play all over the world, some placing the pursuit of individual glory before national pride. How many times have we seen a footballer kiss the badge on his shirt, only to hand in a transfer request the next day? And across the Big Pond American footballers punch their weight on the gridiron, but unlike rugby players, they have all sorts of protective equipment to keep them safe as they go rampaging into the opposition. Without doubt, it is in the sport of Rugby Union that one can find true warriors, icons, gentlemen and transgressors, match-winners, inspirational leaders, brute strength, unrivalled bravery, sublime skills with hand and foot – but, above all else, the one thing that makes a Rugby Union player stand tall above the sporting masses, national pride. A national pride born out of a will to win not for himself but for the country he so proudly represents. For every time a Rugby Union player lines up for his nation he does so knowing that for the next 80 minutes he sacrifices his body for his country in a sport where one tackle can quite easily end even the most promising of careers.

I never played rugby at school, and the only time rugby really crossed my mind was when the Barbarians were playing. I was fascinated with this collection of stars and their exploits against some of the greatest nations in the world, particularly the mighty All Blacks. However, the IRB Rugby World Cup and the Six Nations Championship have propelled Rugby Union into our living-rooms like never before. There was a certain mystique about 30 men doing battle with only their national pride at stake.

If horse racing is "The Sport of Kings", then undoubtedly Rugby Union is "The Sport of Spartans".

**John White**
*December 2008*

## ❧ ENGLAND'S BEST IN CARDIFF ❧

England's 44–15 win over Wales at the Millennium Stadium in the 2001 Six Nations Championship was their highest score and biggest winning margin in Cardiff. In the same game Wales's Neil Jenkins became the first player to score 1,000 points in internationals.

## ❧ THE DARLING OF TWICKENHAM ❧

On 2 January 1982, Erica Roe, a bookshop assistant working in Petersfield, Hampshire, famously ran topless across the pitch at Twickenham during an England versus Australia game. She was accompanied by a friend during her streak, and when Roe was escorted off the field, much to the disappointment of her many admirers in the crowd, a policeman covered her 40-inch chest with his helmet. Following the incident, which she claimed was the result of too much alcohol, she obtained several modelling appearances. Many consider Roe to be Britain's most famous streaker. Erica appeared on the nostalgic television programmes *After They were Famous* (1999) and *80s Mania* (2001).

## ❧ THE ELITE FOUR ❧

Since the inaugural Six Nations in 2000 and up to 2013, only four teams have won the tournament: France four times, England three and Wales twice France five times, England four times, Wales three times and Ireland once, when they claimed the 2009 Grand Slam.

## ❧ ALL SMILES IN DUBLIN ❧

Ireland's victory over France in Dublin in the 2001 Six Nations Championship was their first win over *Les Bleus* in Dublin since 1983. In addition, Ireland had not won their first two games in the Five Nations or Six Nations Championship since 1983.

## ❧ SUPERPOWERS VANQUISHED ❧

In 2005 Wales claimed their first Grand Slam in 27 years. It was also the first time since 2000, when the old Five Nations became Six Nations, that the Championship was not won by either of the northern hemisphere's two superpowers, England and France. Wales beat England 11–9 in Cardiff and France 28–14 in Paris *en route* to the Grand Slam.

## ⚜ IRISH RUGBY ANTHEM ⚜

"The Soldier's Song" was composed in 1907 by Peadar Kearney
with music by Kearney and Patrick Heeney. The Presidential Salute
comprises the first four bars and the last five bars.

### The Soldier's Song (Amhrán na bhFiann)

We'll sing a song, a soldier's song,
With cheering rousing chorus,
As round our blazing fires we throng,
The starry heavens o'er us;
Impatient for the coming fight,
And as we wait the morning's light,
Here in the silence of the night,
We'll chant a soldier's song.
*Chorus*
Soldiers are we, whose lives are pledged to Ireland;
Some have come from a land beyond the wave.
Sworn to be free, no more our ancient sire land
Shall shelter the despot or the slave.
Tonight we man the gap of danger
In Erin's cause, come woe or weal
'Mid cannons' roar and rifles' peal,
We'll chant a soldier's song.

In valley green, on towering crag,
Our fathers fought before us,
And conquered 'neath the same old flag
That's proudly floating o'er us.
We're children of a fighting race,
That never yet has known disgrace,
And as we march, the foe to face,
We'll chant a soldier's song.
*Chorus*
Sons of the Gael! Men of the Pale!
The long watched day is breaking;
The serried ranks of Inisfail
Shall set the Tyrant quaking.
Our camp fires now are burning low;
See in the east a silv'ry glow,
Out yonder waits the Saxon foe,
So chant a soldier's song.

## ✳ A CELTIC SPECTACLE ✳

The 2001 Six Nations Championship witnessed the highest draw in the competition's history when Scotland fought back from a 19-point deficit to claim a dramatic 28–28 draw with Wales at Murrayfield. The half-time score read: Scotland 6, Wales 18.

## ✳ ENGLAND SLAUGHTERED ✳

Ireland, favourites at the start of the 2007 tournament before losing to 20–17 France in their second game, got their Six Nations campaign back on track by thrashing England 43–13 at Croke Park. It was Ireland's record win over England. who played second fiddle to the Irish juggernaut throughout the game. Ireland led 23–3 at the interval following three Ronan O'Gara penalties and tries from Girvan Dempsey and David Wallace (O'Gara converted both). Jonny Wilkinson kicked a penalty for the visitors, who were making their first appearance at Croke Park. England, winners of their opening two games, were simply no match for the guile and work rate of the Irish side. Early in the second half a try from debutant David Strettle cut the deficit to 26–13, but Shane Horgan and Isaac Boss added further tries as England just ran out of ideas and steam. The 30-point winning margin smashed Ireland's all-time record winning margin against England, 22–0 in 1947. The 43 points was the most England had conceded in competition history, surpassing a 37–12 loss to France in Paris in 1972.

## ✳ TWICKENHAM CENTENARY ✳

The 100th anniversary of the first international match played at Twickenham Stadium was celebrated during the 2010 RBS Six Nations Championship. On 6 February 2010, England wore a special commemorative shirt against Wales. England ran out 30–17 winners. The first international match played at Twickenham also saw Wales as the visitors, on 15 January 1910, with England winning 11–6 in what was the inaugural Five Nations Championship.

## ✳ THE TASMANIAN DEVIL ✳

On 2 March 1913, Scotland's Tasmanian-born winger William Stewart scored a record four tries against Ireland. Ireland's current captain, Brian O'Driscoll, scored a hat-trick of tries against Scotland in 2002, and two other Irishmen have notched up hat-tricks in the fixture, Eugene Davy in 1930 and Seamus Byrne in 1953.

## ❧ WIT AND WISDOM OF RUGBY (1) ❧

"We beat France here [the National Stadium, Cardiff] to win the Grand Slam and the Welsh fans were full of praise: 'Oh, you're terrific, Gareth. You're playing better than ever', and I thought to myself, 'This might be a good time to go.'"
*Gareth Edwards, after playing his last ever game for Wales in Cardiff on 18 March 1978*

## ❧ CALCUTTA CUP BECOMES A FOOTBALL ❧

England's lacklustre 9–6 win over Scotland at Murrayfield in the 1988 Five Nations Championship meant England retained the Calcutta Cup. Hours later the famous trophy, which dated back to 1879, was damaged by the antics of some drunken players, including England's Dean Richards and Scotland's John Jeffrey, who decided to use the cup as a football after emptying the whisky it contained over English hooker Brian Moore while walking along Princes Street, Edinburgh. As a consequence of their distasteful behaviour, the England No. 8 was given a one-match ban while Jeffrey was handed a six-month ban from the SRU. It cost the SRU £1,000 to repair the Calcutta Cup.

## ❧ COME IN NUMBER 66 ❧

The 1995 Five Nations Championship was the 66th edition of the tournament since France were invited to join the Home Nations Championship in 1910. England won the Grand Slam for the 11th time in 1995.

## ❧ FOOT-AND-MOUTH ❧

In 2001 the completion of a Six Nations Championship was postponed for the first time since 1962, when foot-and-mouth disease struck Britain. The epidemic resulted in the government imposing severe restrictions on travel, especially between Britain and Ireland, and therefore the decision was taken to postpone Ireland's three fixtures against the home nations until the infectious outbreak was under control. Ireland finally played their games in September and October, with England retaining their Six Nations crown but missing out on the coveted Grand Slam after losing 20–14 to Ireland at Lansdowne Road, Dublin, on 20 October 2001. Italy propped up the table for the second year in a row.

# ❦ GARETH EDWARDS – SIMPLY THE BEST ❧

Gareth Owen Edwards was born on 12 July 1947 in Pontardawe, Wales. A miner's son from Gwaun-cae-Gurwen (his father was named Granville), Gareth won a scholarship to Millfield School in Somerset, where he came under the tutelage of PE teacher Bill Samuels. He made his debut for Wales, aged 19, on 1 April 1967 in Wales's 20–14 loss to France at the Colombes Stadium, Paris. It was an inauspicious start to his international career – both his passing and his tactical kicking came under fire from the critics. France went on to win the title in 1967, while Wales took the wooden spoon. Within a year, aged 20, Edwards became Wales's youngest ever captain, and he was the linchpin in the Welsh side that enjoyed a golden age of rugby during the 1970s. During his international career, between 1967 and 1978, Wales dominated the Five Nations Championship, winning the title seven times, including five Triple Crowns and three Grand Slams. Edwards was part of a mighty Welsh and British Lions back-line that included legends of the sport such as John Bevan, Gerald Davies, John Dawes, Barry John and J. P. R. Williams. Indeed, the half-back partnership that Edwards formed with Barry John was crucial to Wales's success during the 1970s.

Edwards played 53 times for Wales, all consecutive, including 13 as captain, and scored 20 tries in addition to winning 10 Test caps during a British Lions career, from 1968 to 1974, which included two Test series victories over New Zealand and South Africa. The 1971 British Lions became the first Lions side to win a Test series in New Zealand, and the 1974 Lions were unbeaten in South Africa. He simply had it all – blistering speed, tremendous strength, agility, skill, vision and guile. In November 2002 he was named as the greatest Welsh player of all time in a poll conducted by the *Western Mail*, *South Wales Echo*, *Wales on Sunday* and nine Celtic Press titles.

On 18 March 1978, he played his final international for Wales, a 16–7 win over France in the National Stadium, Cardiff, which gave Wales the Five Nations Championship crown and the Grand Slam. In a poll of international rugby players conducted in 2003 by *Rugby World* magazine, Edwards was declared the greatest player of all time – and few would disagree. In the 2007 New Year Honours list he was awarded a CBE for his services to rugby. Today he commentates on rugby matches for the BBC and S4C, while a statue of Gareth Edwards stands in the St David's Shopping Centre in Cardiff.

## *Did You Know That?*
Gareth Edwards did not miss an international for Wales through injury.

## ✣ EPIC GAMES (1) ✣

### 1903 – WALES 21, ENGLAND 5

The turn of the twentieth century also saw a golden age for Welsh rugby, with Wales winning the Home Nations Championship (France did not enter proceedings until 1910) five times in the first decade. Although it was Scotland who won the Championship and Triple Crown in 1903, this game played at Swansea will not only be remembered for the 21–5 win over the English, but also for the feat of a certain Jehoida Hodges. An injury to Wales's regular wing three-quarter resulted in Hodges, a prop forward, being asked to fill the void, and fill it he did, running in a hat-trick of tries.

*Did You Know That?*
In the first decade of the twentieth century, England won the wooden spoon five times (1901, 1903, 1905, 1906 and 1907).

## ✣ FULL OF HOT AIR ✣

During the early days of the sport, rugby balls were crafted from freshly harvested pigs' bladders that were inflated through the stem of a clay pipe. The balls were then encased in leather by Rugby School's local cobbler, William Gilbert, and blown up by his nephew, James. In 1870, Richard Lindon, a ball manufacturer, began producing inflatable rubber bladders after his wife died from a disease caught while blowing up a pig's bladder. The original leather-encased rugby balls were prone to waterlogging and amazingly were only replaced in the 1980s by waterproof synthetics. Although the Gilbert family is no longer involved in the making of the ball, the name lives on as the No. 1 choice for Six Nations Championship games.

*Did You Know That?*
The RFU made the ovalness of the ball compulsory in 1892.

## ✣ LOCK, STOCK AND ATTACK ✣

Scotland's Alistair McHarg (44 caps, 1968–79) ended up in areas of the pitch where locks normally dared not go, quite often appearing on the wing, sometimes helping out as third centre and, on occasion, as an auxiliary full-back. His partnership with Gordon Brown (30 caps, 1969–76) in the second row is one of the best ever pairings in a position where the Scots have always been strong. During his club career he played for West of Scotland and London Scottish.

## RUGBY'S ROYAL ASSOCIATION

English Rugby Union has witnessed several relationships with royalty. In 1936, Russian émigré Prince Obolensky scored two tries in England's first win over the All Blacks. During the 1980s England captain Will Carling was romantically linked with the late Princess of Wales. In 1988 a Nigerian prince, Andrew Harriman, won his first and only cap for England playing on the wing against Australia. Coach Clive Woodward made Prince Harry the England mascot during their successful World Cup-winning campaign in 2003, and his brother, Prince William, the British Lions mascot during their tour of New Zealand in 2005 (lost 3–0). Today the relationship between England's outside centre Mike Tindall and the Princess Royal's daughter, Zara Phillips, is never far from the media's attention.

## MOST POINTS IN FIVE/SIX NATIONS

557 ◆ Ronan O'Gara, Ireland
546 ◆ Jonny Wilkinson, England
467 ◆ Stephen Jones, Wales
406 ◆ Neil Jenkins, Wales
403 ◆ Chris Paterson, Scotland

## IF YOU KNOW YOUR HISTORY – 1

In 1871 England and Scotland played the first Rugby Union international.

## ELVIS LEAVES THE BUILDING

On 17 March 2007, France's Elvis Vermeulen touched down in the final minute of his nation's game against Scotland at the Stade de France, Paris. His try gave the French the 27-point victory over the Scots they required to secure the Six Nations Championship title on points difference – France finishing on +69, Ireland on +65.

***Did You Know That?***
South African Craig Joubert, the match referee, referred Vermeulen's try to the television match official (TMO), who just happened to be an Irishman, and asked him to consider whether there was any reason why the try should not be awarded. The TMO advised that there was no reason, and the referee awarded the try.

# 𝕝 GRAND SLAMS (1) – WALES 1908 𝕝

Wales won the first Grand Slam in the four-nation competition in 1908 – France only entered in 1910. Nevertheless, having beaten England 28–18 at foggy Bristol and Scotland 6–5 at Swansea, Wales did play France in a friendly at Cardiff and inflicted a crushing 36–4 victory. The championship decider was against Ireland in Belfast and Wales triumphed 11–5, courtesy of two late tries from Reggie Gibbs and Johnnie Williams. Uniquely, Wales had a different captain in all four matches.

### HOME NATIONS CHAMPIONSHIP 1908

| Team | P | W | D | L | PF | PA | Pts |
|------|---|---|---|---|----|----|-----|
| Wales | 3 | 3 | 0 | 0 | 45 | 28 | 6 |
| Scotland | 3 | 1 | 0 | 2 | 32 | 32 | 2 |
| England | 3 | 1 | 0 | 2 | 41 | 47 | 2 |
| Ireland | 3 | 1 | 0 | 2 | 24 | 35 | 2 |

### RESULTS 1908

| Date | Venue | Opponent | Score | Captains |
|------|-------|----------|-------|----------|
| 18 January | Bristol | England | 28–18 | AF Harding |
| 1 February | Swansea | Scotland | 6–5 | G Travers |
| *2 March | Cardiff | France | 36–4 | ET Morgan |
| 14 March | Belfast | Ireland | 11–5 | H Winfield |

* *Friendly international – the first ever between Wales and France.*

### *Did You Know That?*
The Wales v France match in Cardiff was their first ever meeting and it came two years before France joined the Championship.

# 𝕝 A SHIFT IN POWER 𝕝

Wales's Six Nations Championship success in 2005 (Grand Slam winners) was also only the second time in 11 years (Scotland won in 1999) that England or France were not crowned champions. England won the crown in 2000, 2001 and 2003 (Grand Slam winners), while the French took the Grand Slam in 2002 and 2004.

### *Did You Know That?*
Wales's famous 24–18 comeback win in Paris over France in the 2005 Six Nations Championship denied the French a third Grand Slam in four years.

## ✒ WIT AND WISDOM OF RUGBY (2) ✒

"[Barry] John ran in another dimension of time and space. His opponents ran into the glass walls which covered his escape routes from their bewildered clutches. He left mouths, and back rows, agape."
*Dai Smith and Gareth Williams, writing about Barry John in* The Official History of the Welsh Rugby Union

## ✒ SUPERPOWERS DRAW LEVEL ✒

After the 2005 Six Nations Championship, won by Wales (Grand Slam winners), both England and France had won 22 and lost 8 of their 30 matches since Italy were invited to participate in the tournament in 2000.

## ✒ ALL ON THE LINE IN CARDIFF ✒

Going into their final game of the 2008 Six Nations Championship against France at the Millennium Stadium, Wales sat proudly at the top of the table with a two-point lead over the French, having won their previous four games (France lost 24–13 to England in Game 3). France, with a points difference of +27, needed to beat Wales, who were on +65, by 20 points or more in Cardiff to win the Six Nations Championship title. If France won by 19 points, the two teams would be level on points difference but the team with the most tries in the tournament would then claim overall victory. Prior to the match-up both nations had scored 11 tries. Therefore, if the two nations could still not be separated then the title would be shared. The Welsh, cheered on by a partisan home crowd (74,609), knew that a win would not only guarantee them the 2008 Six Nations Championship title but also the coveted Grand Slam. Wales won the game 29–12.

## ✒ THE FATHER OF RUGBY ✒

Had it not been for William Webb Ellis, the game of rugby might never have been invented. In 1823 he picked up a football at Rugby School and made the other boys chase and tackle him. There is a commemorative plaque at Rugby School which reads: "With a fine disregard for the rules of the game of football (soccer) as played in his time, he [William Webb Ellis] first took the ball in his arms and ran with it."

## SCOTS CLAIM FINAL FIVE NATIONS TITLE

In 1999 Scotland claimed the honour of winning the last ever Five Nations Championship title, with Italy invited to join in 2000 and make it the Six Nations.

## THE CABBAGE PATCH

Twickenham is affectionately known as the Cabbage Patch, because the site on which the stadium was built used to be a 10-acre patch of ground where cabbages and other vegetables were grown, along with fruit trees and mushrooms.

## WHEN THE DRAGON ROARED

Welsh fly-half Phil Bennett will always be remembered for his famous team talk to his Welsh team-mates prior to facing the English enemy at the National Stadium, Cardiff, on 5 March 1977: "Look what these bastards have done to Wales. They've taken our coal, our water, our steel. They buy our homes and live in them for a fortnight every year. What have they given us? Absolutely nothing. We've been exploited, raped, controlled and punished by the English – and that's who you are playing this afternoon." Wales won the game 14–9 and clinched the Grand Slam.

## ENGLAND'S DUBLIN DELIGHT

In 2003 England claimed their first Grand Slam title in eight years when they beat Ireland 42–6 at Lansdowne Road, Dublin, in the final game of the 2003 Six Nations tournament. They also became the first nation to win a Grand Slam title away from home in a game where both nations were vying for the coveted prize.

## THE GREEN PIMPERNEL

John Wilson Kyle won 46 caps for Ireland between 1946 and 1958, mainly at fly-half. In 1948 his inspiration on the field guided the Irish to Grand Slam success in the Five Nations Championship. Kyle went on tour with the 1950 Lions in Australia (lost 2–0) and New Zealand (lost 3–0 with one draw), and when he retired in 1958 his caps tally was a world record at the time. On 24 January 1953, Kyle scored a magnificent solo try for Ireland at Ravenhill, Belfast, in their 16–3 win over France in the Five Nations Championship.

## 𝕏 ENGLAND AND WALES NECK AND NECK 𝕏

The tournament was first contested in 1883, with just the four home nations – England, Ireland, Scotland and Wales – competing. In the early years, there were a number of controversies and not every edition was completed. France joined the competition in 1910, but withdrew after 1931, only rejoining it after the hiatus for World War 2 – World War 1 had resulted in no Five Nations 1915–19. The newcomers are Italy, who joined only in 2000. Overall, England and Wales have enjoyed the most success, with 26 outright wins each (Wales have shared 11, England ten). England, however, have 12 Grand Slams and 23 Triple Crowns to Wales's 11 and 20, respectively. France, who have played 1910–31 and 1947–date, lie third with 17 titles (eight shared) and nine Grand Slams. Scotland have 14 titles (eight shared), three Grand Slams and ten Triple Crowns. Ireland is the least successful of the original four home nations, with 11 titles (eight shared), two Grand Slams and ten Triple Crowns. Italy have no championships to their name and have a best finish of fourth (in 2007 and 2013).

## 𝕏 THE COTTON TRADERS 𝕏

Fran Cotton won 31 caps for England between 1971 and 1981, three as captain of the national side. In 1987 he founded the company Cotton Traders along with former Sale and England team-mate, Steve Smith.

## 𝕏 GALLIC DOMINATION OF THE 1980S 𝕏

During the 1980s, France won the Five Nations Championship six times (three shared), including two Grand Slams (1981 and 1987). Their success was very much based around their massive pack, while their coach Jacques Fouroux had at his disposal some of the greatest players ever to represent France, including Serge Blanco, Philippe Sella and Daniel Dubroca. Dubroca not only captained his country at the inaugural Rugby World Cup finals in 1987 but actually replaced Fouroux as national team coach in 1990 following Fouroux's resignation. Fouroux was the French captain when they won their second Grand Slam title in 1977.

### Did You Know That?
After France lost 19–10 to England in the 1991 Rugby World Cup quarter-finals, Dubroca manhandled the referee, David Bishop, after the final whistle was blown and accused Bishop of being a cheat.

## ❦ IT ALL ENDED IN CONTROVERSY ❧

Round 4 of the 2007 RBS Six Nations Championship saw Italy record a second victory in the same tournament for the first time, defeating the Welsh 23–20 in Rome in a game that ended in controversy. Going into the closing stages of the encounter in the Stadio Flaminio, Wales trailed the Italians by three points. However, the Welsh had the opportunity of drawing level when they were awarded a kickable penalty near the Italian 22-metre line. The referee informed the Welsh that 10 seconds remained on the game clock, and so they chose to kick for touch, thinking they would then be able to regroup and plan an attacking line-out to bring a possible try-scoring and ultimately game-winning opportunity. However, to the utter disbelief of the Wales players the referee blew his whistle for final time before the Welsh could even organize a line-out. Naturally, the Welsh players were incensed, but the 23–20 result stood. The referee later apologized for the misunderstanding that had arisen.

## ❦ WOULD-BE BONUS-POINT CHAMPS ❧

In 2002 France won the RBS Six Nations Championship Grand Slam, with England finishing runners-up on eight points, their only defeat coming against the French, a 20–15 reverse at the Stade de France, Paris. However, if the bonus-point system – which the Six Nations does not use – had been applied (as it is in most other domestic rugby competitions and in the pool stages of the IRB World Cup since 2003), it would have made a major difference. Under the bonus-point system, points are awarded as follows: four for a win, two for a draw, and none for a loss by eight points or more. However, one bonus point is awarded both for scoring four or more tries (regardless of the result) and for a loss by seven points or fewer. Under that points system, both England and France would have amassed 21 points, but England had a +131 points difference and France +81, so England would have been crowned Six Nations champions despite France's Grand Slam.

## ❦ OUTDONE BY HIS SISTER ❧

Craig "Minto" Chalmers was capped 60 times by Scotland, almost always at fly-half, and won one Test cap for the British Lions in 1989 against the Wallabies (the Lions won the series 2–1). However, Craig is not the most capped Scot in his family – his sister Paula Chalmers won more caps playing for the Scottish women's rugby team.

## ❧ A HISTORIC SEASON ❧

England's historic 2001 Grand Slam-winning season also witnessed a record-breaking campaign. Coach Clive Woodward's side scored the most team points in a season, a staggering 229 points from their five matches. England also scored the most team tries for a Six Nations Championship campaign, an incredible 29 tries. Their 80–23 win over Italy was a record score (123 points) and a record winning margin (57 points). Jonny Wilkinson scored 35 of England's 80 points in the demolition of Italy, the highest number of points scored by a player in a game, and amassed 89 points in the campaign, the highest total ever achieved in the Six Nations Championship.

## ❧ MOST TRIES IN A TOURNAMENT ❧

During the 1914 Five Nations Championship, England's Cyril Lowe scored a record eight tries in helping England secure the Grand Slam, a record only matched by Ian Smith of Scotland in 1925, when the Scots also won the Grand Slam.

## ❧ PLAYERS NUMBERED ❧

In 1921 the Rugby Football Union (RFU) celebrated its Jubilee Year (50th anniversary), while the International Rugby Board (IRB) took the decision to introduce numbering on players' jerseys. Numbers 1 to 15 were used, as is the case today.

## ❧ OVER AND OUT FOR JOHNSON ❧

In 2000 an Achilles' tendon injury forced England's captain Martin Johnson to miss the entire inaugural Six Nations Championship campaign, but on his return he helped his club, Leicester Tigers, win the Premiership title.

## ❧ THE MILLENNIUM TROPHY ❧

The Millennium Trophy, or *Corn an Mhílaoise* in Gaelic, was introduced in 1988 and is contested annually by England and Ireland when they meet in the Six Nations Championship. The trophy, in the shape of a horned Viking helmet, was commissioned as part of Dublin's millennial celebrations in 1988 and was donated by Digital. The inaugural competition in 1988 did not form part of that year's Five Nations Championship.

## ⚤ THE SIX NATIONS TROPHY ⚤

The idea of a trophy for the Five Nations (now Six Nations) Championship was first thought of by Lord Burghersh in 1992 and was first presented to France, the winners in 1993. Lord Burghersh organized an exhibition of British national sporting trophies in 1992, featuring trophies such as the Ashes urn (cricket), the FA Cup (football), the Ryder Cup (golf) and the Wimbledon trophies (tennis). His Lordship quickly realized that the only major sporting competition in which a British side competed that did not present a trophy to the winners was Rugby Union's Five Nations Championship. He subsequently commissioned the design and production of a trophy, which then featured as the centrepiece of the exhibition, and afterwards he presented it to the Five Nations committee. The Six Nations trophy is held in trust by the Six Nations Championship Trophy Trust.

## ⚤ CLOSE ENCOUNTERS IN ROME ⚤

England's four-point margin of victory (19–15) over Italy on 11 February 2012 in the Stadio Olimpico, Rome, matched the closest Italy has ever come to beating England. Rob Webber made his England international debut in this match. England also beat Italy by four points, 23–19, at Rome's Stadio Flaminio, in 2008.

## ⚤ THE DRAGONFLY KING ⚤

During the British Lions' unprecedented 1971 tour victory in New Zealand the performances of the legendary Welsh fly-half, Barry John, nicknamed "the King" by the All Blacks on that tour, were so mesmeric that one journalist wrote: "John was the dragonfly on the anvil of destruction." Indeed, his ruthless kicking display in the first Test against the All Blacks' distinguished full-back, and the one man the Lions feared most, Fergie McCormick, was so majestic, and McCormick's public humiliation at the hands and feet of the King so comprehensive, that he was dropped and was never selected again.

## ⚤ A MODERN CORINTHIAN ⚤

When Jean-Pierre Rives (1975–84) retired from international rugby he released an autobiography entitled *A Modern Corinthian*. No one argued with this adieu from the sport Rives graced as magnificently as his long blond locks fluttered in the breeze every time he picked up the ball for *Les Bleus*.

# ❧ FANTASY TEAMS – ENGLAND XV ☙

```
            1          2          3
          Phil       Phil      Jason
        VICKERY   GREENING   LEONARD

            4          5
      6   Martin      Bill    7
    Richard JOHNSON  BEAUMONT Neil
     HILL   (capt)    8      BACK
                   Lawrence
                  DALLAGLIO

            9         10
          Matt      Jonny
        DAWSON    WILKINSON

    11        12        13        14
  Jason     Jeremy     Will     Rory
ROBINSON  GUSCOTT   CARLING  UNDERWOOD

            15
          Dusty
          HARE
```

*Replacements*
16 Josh *LEWSEY* ❖ 17 David *DUCKHAM* ❖ 18 Dean *RICHARDS*
19 Wade *DOOLEY* ❖ 20 Gareth *CHILCOTT* ❖ 21 Brian *MOORE*
22 Graham *ROWNTREE* ❖ 23 Mike *TINDALL*
*Coach*
Sir Clive *WOODWARD*

***Did You Know That?***
Sir Clive Woodward became the first coach of a Rugby Union team
to be knighted.

## ❧ THE WELSH CENTURIONS ☙

The Welsh Rugby Union awards a special commemorative cap to
players who have won 50 Test caps for the Principality. While there
have been 30 players who have won this award, only three of them
reached a century of caps for Wales. Gethin Jenkins, Wales's most-
capped prop forward, is knocking on the door of this elite club. He
finished the 2013 Six Nations Chanpionship on 98 caps.

104 ❖ Stephen Jones (1998–2011)
100 ❖ Gareth Thomas (1995–2007)
100 ❖ Martyn Williams (1996–2012)

## ❧ SCOTLAND RUGBY ANTHEM ❧

Although Scotland does not have an official national anthem, "Flower of Scotland" has been sung before Scotland's international matches since 1990. It was written in 1967 by Roy Williamson of the folk group the Corries and tells the story of the victory of the Scots, led by King Robert the Bruce, over Edward II of England at the Battle of Bannockburn in 1314.

**Flower of Scotland (Flùr na h-Alba)**
O Flower of Scotland,
When will we see
Your like again,
That fought and died for
Your wee bit Hill and Glen,
And stood against him,
Proud Edward's army,
And sent him homeward,
Tae think again.

The hills are bare now,
And autum leaves lie thick and still,
O'er land that is lost now,
Which those so dearly held,
And stood against him,
Proud Edward's army,
And sent him homeward,
Tae think again.

Those days are past now,
And in the past
They must remain,
But we can still rise now,
And be the nation again,
That stood against him,
Proud Edward's army,
And sent him homeward,
Tae think again.

## ❧ CAPTAIN O'GARA ❧

On 15 March 2008, Ronan O'Gara captained Ireland for the first time, losing 33–10 away to England in the Six Nations Championship.

## ✌ WIT AND WISDOM OF RUGBY (3) ✌

"If I stand on a hill I can see England."
*John Jeffrey reveals his only regret about his farm being in the Borders*

## ✌ IT'S YOUR TRY, MY FRIEND ✌

In their opening game of the 2008 RBS Six Nations Championship, Italy lost 16–11 to Ireland at Croke Park, Dublin. During the game, Italy's solitary try was credited to Sergio Parisse, but after the match had ended, Parisse admitted that the try had in fact been scored by Martin Castrogio.

## ✌ DROP GOAL HISTORY MADE ✌

On 23 February 2008, England fly-half Jonny Wilkinson broke the world record for drop goals when he scored his 29th at the Stade de France against France in England's 24–13 RBS Six Nations Championship win. He previously shared the record with Hugo Porta of Argentina. Jonny's tally at the end of the game stood at 1,023 points: from his world record 29 drop goals, 6 tries, 144 conversions and 206 penalty goals.

*Did You Know That?*
Jonny dropped his first goal against South Africa in the summer of 2000 in his 20th appearance for his country.

## ✌ THE TRIPLE CROWN ✌

The Triple Crown is part of the Six Nations Championship, but is contested by only the four home nations, namely England, Ireland, Scotland and Wales. Unlike the Grand Slam, which requires a five-match sweep by a country, the Triple Crown is won only if a country defeats the three home nations. There was no physical trophy until the tournament's main sponsors, RBS, commissioned one in 2006.

**England** (23): 1883, 1884, 1892, 1913, 1914, 1921, 1923, 1924,
1928, 1934, 1937, 1954, 1957, 1960, 1980, 1991, 1992, 1995,
1996, 1997, 1998, 2002, 2003
**Wales** (20): 1893, 1900, 1902, 1905, 1908, 1909, 1911, 1950, 1952,
1965, 1969, 1971, 1976, 1977, 1978, 1979, 1988, 2005, 2008, 2012
**Scotland** (10): 1891, 1895, 1901, 1903, 1907, 1925, 1933, 1938, 1984, 1990
**Ireland** (10): 1894, 1899, 1948, 1949, 1982, 1985, 2004, 2006, 2007, 2009

## ❧ EPIC GAMES (2) ❧

### 1925 – SCOTLAND 14, ENGLAND 11

On 1 March 1925, Scotland celebrated the opening of their new ground, Murrayfield, beating England 14–11 to claim the Calcutta Cup (for the first time for 13 years), the Triple Crown and their first ever Grand Slam title. Going into the last minutes of a pulsating encounter England led 11–10, but Scotland scored a match-winning try, much to the delight of the partisan home crowd.

## ❧ BBC SPORTS PERSONALITY OF THE YEAR ❧

The BBC Sports Personality of the Year Award is voted for by the general public towards the end of the calendar year, and is presented to the outstanding sportsman or sportswoman from that year. It is one of the most prestigious all-sport awards in British sport and dates back to 1954, when the long-distance runner, Chris Chattaway, took the honours. Only one rugby player has ever won the coveted prize, England's Jonny Wilkinson in 2003, with his team-mate, Martin Johnson, coming second. Other rugby players who have featured in the top three are:

1971  Barry John.............................Third (HRH Princess Anne was the winner)
1974  Willie John McBride.................Third (Brendan Foster was the winner)
1991  Will Carling.........Runner-up to Liz McColgan (long-distance runner)

## ❧ KING OF THE KICKERS ❧

Rodney Webb, the man who developed the modern rugby ball, once stated that he believed that Barry John was the greatest kicker of all time. Webb pointed out that the modern rugby ball is prevented from soaking up water by a special coating similar to the laminate that is used on the hulls of giant oil tankers. The ball used in the 1960s and 1970s, when John tortured teams, soaked up water and often plopped down on extremely muddy surfaces, soaking up even more moisture.

## ❧ EARLY DAYS ❧

Rugby was introduced in Italy sometime between 1890 and 1895, when British communities first played the game in Genoa. The first documented Rugby Union match played in Italy occurred in 1910, when a demonstration game was played in Turin between Racing Club of Paris and Servette of Geneva.

## ❧ BARRY JOHN – THE KING ❧

Barry John was born on 6 January 1946 in Cefneithin, South Wales. The young John attended Gwendraeth Grammar School in the Gwendraeth Valley, north of Llanelli. He made his international debut for Wales against Australia at Cardiff Arms Park on 3 December 1966, coming on at fly-half as a replacement for David Watkins.

After two largely unsuccessful seasons, John enjoyed his first real success in 1968 and was selected for the British Lions tour of South Africa, although he broke his collarbone in the first Test. In 1969, John helped Wales to the Five Nations Championship and the Triple Crown (an 8–8 draw in France cost them the Grand Slam). John was part of a magical Welsh back division that ushered in a golden age for the Principality. His half-back partnership with Gareth Edwards was pivotal in Wales's success, and many considered John to be the best rugby player in the world in the years 1970–72. He teased and tormented teams in equal measure and ghosted through defences with consummate ease.

In January 1971, John began to take Wales's goal kicks and he turned out to be a superb kicker. John and Wales won the Grand Slam in 1971 and he was an obvious selection for that summer's British Lions tour to New Zealand. The Lions won their first ever series against the All Blacks and John made 20 of his first 24 conversion attempts, scoring a record 188 points in all matches and 30 of the Lions' 48 points in the four Tests. Many consider the 1971 Lions tour to be the pinnacle of his career. The All Blacks nicknamed him "The King", although it was Edwards who became the greatest rugby player the world has ever seen.

Perhaps Barry John's greatest moment in a Welsh jersey came on 27 March 1971, when Wales visited the Stade Colombes, to face France in the final Five Nations match of that season. Wales were already assured of winning the title, and had secured the Triple Crown, but France provided a stubborn opponent on the day until John broke through their defence to score and help Wales to a 9–5 win. However, less than a year later the willowy John announced his retirement at the age of just 27, citing constant media attention as the main reason for him falling out of love with the game. He played his final game for Wales on 25 February 1972 in the National Stadium, Cardiff, in a 20–6 Five Nations Championship win over France. And so, after 25 Welsh caps and five appearances for the British Lions, John left the public arena, and just as he so often had been with defences all around the world, suddenly he was out of sight.

### Did You Know That?
A story is that John quit rugby shortly after a young girl, in deference to his royal nickname, curtsied to him outside a local bank.

## ❧ BBC SCOTLAND'S BEST ❧

The BBC Scotland Sports Personality of the Year Award is the most prestigious annual sport award in Scotland and was first presented in 1977 when Kenny Dalglish (football) claimed the honours. Since then only two rugby players have won: David Sole in 1980 and Gavin Hastings in 1995.

## ❧ ENGLAND'S FIRST IN FIVE YEARS ❧

England's 33–10 win over Ireland at Twickenham in the 2008 RBS Six Nations Championship was their first Millennium Trophy success over the Irish in five years.

## ❧ NO LUCK FOR THE IRISH ❧

After France were presented with the inaugural trophy for winning the Five Nations Championship in 1993, Wales were winners in 1994, England in 1995 and 1996, France again in 1997 and 1998, and Scotland won it in 1999. Ireland did not get another chance to win the Five Nations Championship trophy, because Italy joined the competition in 2000 and the tournament became known as the "Six Nations Championship".

## ❧ THE FRENCH GIANT ❧

France's giant centre Yannick Jauzion, who helped his country to the Five Nations Championship and Grand Slam glory in 2002 and 2004, was a member of the Toulouse team that reached the Heineken Cup final in 2003, 2004 and 2005, winning the 2005 Man of the Match Award following Toulouse's win over Stade Français. Despite his size (6 ft 4 ins) and bulk (16 st 10 lbs), Jauzion is a player of tremendous speed and flair. He was first capped in 2001 and won his 50th cap in 2008.

## ❧ MASSIMO THE GREAT ❧

Massimo Cuttitta won 69 caps for Italy, 22 of them as captain, and scored 29 points. He made his debut for the *Azzurri* on 7 April 1990 against Poland, and played his final game on 18 March 2000, when Italy lost 59–12 to England at the Stadio Flaminio in their maiden Six Nations Championship. Massimo grew up in South Africa with his twin brother Marcello, another Italian international winger.

## ✆ JONNY BEATS ROB ✆

Jonny Wilkinson holds the record for the highest number of points scored in a single Calcutta Cup match, amassing 27 points in 2007. Wilkinson beat fellow countryman Rob Andrew's previous best tally of 24 points.

## ✆ IBANEZ ELEVATED ✆

When France's regular captain, Fabien Pelous, was out injured for his nation's first two matches of the 2007 RBS Six Nations Championship against Italy and Ireland, the vice-captain Raphael Ibanez was elevated to the captaincy for both matches. Pelous's injury ultimately ruled him out of the entire 2007 competition.

## ✆ KICKING IT ✆

England's Jonny Wilkinson appeared with the England football team captain, David Beckham, in the *Kicking It* television advertisements for Adidas prior to the 2003 Rugby World Cup finals in Australia.

## ✆ WOODEN SPOON BLUES ✆

Thirteen out of the first 14 Six Nations Championships wooden spoons went to teams in blue, France (one), Scotland (three) and Italy (nine). Wales, who wear red, had that unwanted distinction in 2003.

## ✆ THE DYNAMIC DUO ✆

Wales's greatest ever half-back partnership of Gareth Edwards and Barry John was crucial to the golden age enjoyed by Welsh rugby during the 1970s. Edwards and John shared a tight bond, forged at an early Welsh training session, when John suggested to Edwards a revolutionary new attacking strategy: "You throw 'em, I'll catch 'em." The words have entered Welsh folklore. Indeed, their understanding of each other was quite extraordinary – and the pair very often spoke to each other in Welsh during international matches, particularly in games against England, leaving the opposition scratching their heads as to what the dynamic duo had just planned. On the odd occasion the pair were wrongly punished by over-zealous referees who thought they were being sworn at in Welsh! Edwards and John were simply so good that no set of backs since, regardless of nationality, have ever been able to match them for attacking spirit and verve.

## *O*

## ❧ IF YOU KNOW YOUR HISTORY – 2 ❧

After 12 years of occasional friendly matches between the four home nations of England, Ireland, Scotland and Wales, the inaugural Home International Championships was played in 1883.

## ❧ THE WOODEN SPOON ❧

The last-placed nation at the end of a Six Nations Championship is said to have won the wooden spoon, although this is merely a figure of speech, as no wooden spoon is presented. The wooden spoon was originally associated with the Mathematical Tripos at Cambridge University and was a booby prize awarded by the students to the person who achieved the lowest exam marks while still managing to obtain a third-class degree. The custom dates back to the early nineteenth century and was discontinued after 1909 when the university began to publish exam results in alphabetical as opposed to score order. Most historians are in doubt about how the Cambridge wooden spoon idea came to be used in Rugby Union, but the generally accepted explanation is that many Cambridge graduates played in the early Home International Championships (England, Ireland, Scotland and Wales), and after 1909 these students may have liked the idea of preserving the concept of the wooden spoon.

## ❧ THE PRINCE OF CENTRES ❧

England coach Clive Woodward called Jeremy Guscott "the Prince of Centres".

## ❧ FIRST SIX NATIONS WINNERS ❧

England were the first nation to win the Six Nations Championship trophy, winning the inaugural tournament in 2000.

## ❧ LES MISÉRABLES ❧

France lost only one game *en route* to winning the 1989 Five Nations Championship, an 11–0 defeat by England at Twickenham. England's win turned out to be the first of eight consecutive losses for the French to Will Carling's teams. It was not until the 1995 Rugby World Cup in South Africa that their terrible run against England came to an end, when they won the third-place play-off match 19–9 in Loftus Versfeld Stadium, Pretoria.

# ❦ GRAND SLAMS (2) – ENGLAND 1913 ❧

England's first Grand Slam came with some ease, built on immaculate defence. In four matches, England conceded just four points, a drop goal, on their trip to Dublin. A 12–0 defeat of Wales in Cardiff was followed by a comprehensive 20–0 drubbing of France at Twickenham. After winning 15–4 against Ireland, the first of two consecutive Grand Slams was completed with a 3–0 Calcutta Cup victory over Scotland at Twickenham. France failed to pick up a win for the third year out of four.

### FIVE NATIONS CHAMPIONSHIP 1913

| Team | P | W | D | L | PF | PA | Pts |
|------|---|---|---|---|----|----|----|
| England | 4 | 4 | 0 | 0 | 50 | 4 | 8 |
| Wales | 4 | 3 | 0 | 1 | 35 | 33 | 6 |
| Scotland | 4 | 2 | 0 | 2 | 50 | 28 | 4 |
| Ireland | 4 | 1 | 0 | 3 | 55 | 60 | 2 |
| France | 4 | 0 | 0 | 4 | 11 | 76 | 0 |

### RESULTS 1908

| Date | Venue | Opponent | Score | Captains |
|------|-------|----------|-------|----------|
| 18 January | Cardiff | Wales | 12–0 | R Poulton |
| 25 January | Twickenham | France | 20–0 | R Poulton |
| 8 February | Dublin | Ireland | 15–4 | R Poulton |
| 15 March | Twickenham | Scotland | 3–0 | R Poulton |

## Did You Know That?
Drop goals were worth four points until just after the Second World War. The value of a try was only three points until the early 1970s and was four points for around 20 years.

# ❦ JONNY'S GONG ❧

On 31 December 2002, England's Jonny Wilkinson was awarded an MBE in the 2003 New Year Honours list. Wilkinson, aged 23, became the youngest Rugby Union player to be honoured, the previous youngest having been the legendary Gareth Edwards, who was 27 when he received his MBE. At the time Jonny had scored 584 points for England, more than any other player. "I am clearly delighted to have been honoured in this way. It is such a prestigious decoration and it comes as something of a shock, to say the least," said Wilkinson. Jonny also holds the Rugby World Cup points scoring record with 277.

## ⚜ JONNY IN PRINT ⚜

As well as being an occasional columnist for *The Times* newspaper Jonny Wilkinson has also written or co-written five books: *Lions and Falcons: My Diary of a Remarkable Year* (Headline, 2001), *My World* (Headline, 2004), *How to Play Rugby My Way* (Headline, 2005), *Tackling Life: Striving for Perfection* (Headline, 2008) and *Jonny: My Autobiography* (Headline, 2011).

*Did You Know That?*
Wilkinson's 2005 book accompanied the BBC series *Jonny's Hotshots*.

## ⚜ FRANCE NICK THE TROPHY ⚜

France won the eighth edition of the RBS Six Nations Championship in 2007, thanks to a points difference just four points better than Ireland's. In their final game, an injury-time try by Elvis Vermeulen at the Stade de France gave France a 46–19 victory over Scotland. Ireland did have the consolation of winning a third Triple Crown in four years (having won it in 2004 and 2006).

## ⚜ TAIT SWITCHES CODES ⚜

Alan Tait won 27 caps at full-back and centre for Scotland between 1987 and 1999, scoring 85 points. However, his career was unconventional. After winning his first cap in 1987, he followed his father's (Alan Tait Snr) footsteps by switching codes in 1988 and taking up Rugby League. Tait Jnr appeared in the 1994 and 1995 Rugby League Challenge Cup finals, and won Rugby League caps for both Scotland (4) and Great Britain (16). He returned to Rugby Union in 1997 and later played for the British & Irish Lions.

## ⚜ TWICKENHAM CHOSEN AS NEW HOME ⚜

In 1907 Billy Williams, a member of the Rugby Football Union (RFU), chose a site at Twickenham to be the location for an English Rugby Union stadium. The RFU paid £5,572 12s 6d for the 10-acre site.

## ⚜ 36 ⚜

When he played for Leicester Tigers, 2009–12, England centre Billy Twelvetrees was nicknamed "36". According to his Irish international club-mate Geordan Murphy, his surname sounded like twelve threes.

# ❧ WIT AND WISDOM OF RUGBY (4) ❧

"A bomb under the West car park at Twickenham on an international day would end fascism in England for a generation."
*Philip Toynbee*

## ❧ BIG BILL ❧

William Beaumont, better known as Bill Beaumont, captained England to an unexpected Grand Slam success in the 1980 Five Nations Championship, their first in 23 years. He made his debut for England on 18 January 1975 when he came on as a replacement for Roger Uttley against Ireland at Lansdowne Road, Dublin, in the Five Nations Championship (England lost the game 12–9 and won the wooden spoon that year). In 1977 he toured Fiji (lost 1–0) and New Zealand (lost 3–1) with the British Lions and won three caps. On 21 January 1978, he ran out as England captain for the first time in a game France won 15–6 at the Parc des Princes in the Five Nations Championship. Following England's 1980 Grand Slam triumph, Beaumont captained the British Lions on their 1980 tour to South Africa (lost 3–1) and played in 10 of their 18 games. He was the first English captain of the Lions since Bernard Gadney on the 1936 tour of Argentina. Bill was capped 34 times by England, a record for a lock at the time he retired through injury in 1982, and captained the side on 21 of those occasions. In addition to his England caps he won seven Lions caps and played 15 times for the Barbarians. He never scored, either for England or the Lions. Away from playing the game, Bill was a captain on the popular BBC quiz show *A Question of Sport*, has represented England on the International Rugby Board since 1999, is the honorary president of the rugby charity Wooden Spoon, and acted as tour manger to the British Lions in 2005 when they lost 3–0 to the All Blacks.

### *Did You Know That?*
In 2007 the RFU announced that the winners of the English County Championship would be awarded the Bill Beaumont Cup.

## ❧ SCOTS SLAM HAT-TRICK ❧

In 1990 Scotland claimed their third Grand Slam title (following those of 1925 and 1984) in what was the 61st edition of the Five Nations Championship, the 96th edition including the original Home Nations Championship series.

## 🍂 THE PRINCE AND THE POMP 🍂

On 4 January 1936 a Russian nobleman, Prince Alexander Sergeevich Obolensky, scored two tries on his international debut for England against New Zealand at Twickenham, a match England won 13–0 to record their first ever victory over the All Blacks. Such was his performance that the game is still referred to as "Obo's Match". The Flying Prince, or Obo as he was known, was born in what was then Petrograd (formerly and now once again St Petersburg) at the height of World War 1, on 17 February 1916, the son of Prince Serge Alexandrovitch Obolensky, a serving officer in the Tsar's Imperial Horse Guards, and his wife Princess Luba. In 1917 the Russian Revolution forced the family to flee their homeland and they moved to Muswell Hill, in London. Obo was educated in England, studied at Brasenose College, Oxford, where he won two rugby blues at wing-threequarter, and played for Leicester Tigers from 1934 to 1939. He was awarded British citizenship in 1936 and played three further games for his adopted nation, a 0–0 draw with Wales in Swansea, a 6–3 loss to Ireland at Lansdowne Road and a 9–8 victory over Scotland at Twickenham. When World War 2 broke out in 1939, following the German invasion of Poland, Obo joined the RAF (54 Squadron). On 29 March 1940, aged just 24, he died during a fighter pilot training exercise when his Hawker Hurricane crashed on Martlesham Heath, Suffolk. He was buried at the Ipswich War Cemetery. In 2006 the RFU commemorated the 70th anniversary of "Obo's Match" by naming a large hospitality suite at Twickenham after him and including a feature in the RFU museum's Wall of Fame. In February 2008, Ipswich Borough Council sanctioned a statue in the town centre in his honour. The newly formed Prince Obolensky Memorial Project (POMP) commissioned the statue from the famous sculptor Harry Gray, whose works include the Battle of Britain Memorial at Dover. Obo's statue will stand in Cromwell Square alongside those of Sir Alf Ramsey and Sir Bobby Robson, both past football managers of Ipswich Town and England.

### Did You Know That?
During the introductions before the New Zealand game at Twickenham, the Prince of Wales, soon to be crowned King Edward VIII, asked Obo, "By what right do you play for England?" Obo answered him on the field, becoming an English hero and schoolboy idol before laying down his life for England. Many sports fans still refer to him as "The Prince".

# 🐾 MOST TRIES IN FIVE/SIX NATIONS HISTORY 🐾

26 ❖ Brian O'Driscoll, Ireland
24 ❖ Ian Smith, Scotland
22 ❖ Shane Williams, Wales
18 ❖ Gareth Edwards, Wales
18 ❖ Cyril Lowe, England
18 ❖ Rory Underwood, England

## 🐾 THE GOLDEN BOYS 🐾

Wales totally dominated the Five Nations Championship during the 1970s and ended the decade with seven titles (two shared) out of the nine tournaments played (in 1972 it was not completed), three Grand Slam titles and five Triple Crowns. The Welsh had some truly gifted rugby players during the 1970s, including their inspirational scrum-half Gareth Edwards and full-back J. P. R. Williams.

## 🐾 HIGH FIVES FOR JOHNSON 🐾

Martin Johnson won the Five/Six Nations Championship five times with England: in 1995, 1996, 2000, 2001 and 2003, the last three times as captain of the side.

## 🐾 SEE YOU AT THE PALACE, MATE 🐾

Two former England captains, Bill Beaumont and Lawrence Dallaglio, headed the list of sporting names honoured in the Queen's Birthday Honours list in June 2008. Beaumont received a CBE and Dallaglio an OBE for services to rugby and charity. Beaumont, the vice-chairman of the International Rugby Board, was recognized for his charitable work with rugby's Wooden Spoon Society which helps disadvantaged children in the UK and Ireland. "I was fortunate enough to receive an OBE for playing the game in 1982, and now 26 years later to get this award for other things which I have managed to achieve makes you feel very humble," said Big Bill. Dallaglio, who retired in May 2008, had previously been awarded an MBE in 2003.

*Did You Know That?*
Dallaglio, who spent the whole of his club playing career with Wasps, won 85 England caps, a Rugby World Cup winner's medal, a Grand Slam, five English Championship titles and two Heineken Cups, and went on three tours with the British Lions.

## ❧ ERIN GO BRAGH ❧

In round three of the 2007 RBS Six Nations Championship, England suffered a tournament record defeat when they lost 43–13 to the Irish at Croke Park. It was England's worst scoreline in the history of the tournament, both in the 30-point margin and the number of points conceded.

*Did You Know That?*
This was the first ever game played between Ireland and England in any sport at Croke Park.

## ❧ THE QUIET MAN TURNS KILLER ❧

In August 2004, Marc Cécillon was arrested by French police for murdering his wife, whom he shot in the head with a Magnum revolver in front of 60 people at a house party in Saint Savin, France. On 10 November 2006, he appeared in court and after being found guilty of murder, he was handed a 20-year prison sentence. Cécillon won 46 caps for France between 1988 and 1995, five as captain, and was often referred to as "the Quiet Man of French Rugby".

## ❧ SHANE'S TOURNAMENT ❧

The 2008 RBS Six Nations Championship saw Shane Williams of Wales setting records *en route* to helping his country win the Grand Slam. His two tries against Scotland in a 30–15 win at Cardiff, on 9 February 2008 meant that he became Wales's all-time leading try-scorer in the history of the tournament with 11 tries. He scored four more tries in the tournament to put him on 15, just two tries behind the all-time leading try-scorer in the history of the Six Nations Championship, Ireland's Brian O'Driscoll, who had 17 at the time. Meanwhile, Shane's try against France in Wales's final game was his 41st, making him his country's all-time leading try-scorer (a record he extended to 58 in an international career spanning 2000–11).

## ❧ THE DRAGON KINGS ❧

On 20 March 1999, Gareth Thomas equalled the feat of former Welsh legends Willie Llewellyn, Reggie Gibbs, Maurice Richards, Ieuan Evans and Nigel Walker, when he scored four tries in an international against Italy in Treviso. Thomas achieved the landmark in his 32nd appearance for his country in a match they won 60–21.

## *O*

## ✌ EPIC GAMES (3) ✌

### 1948 – IRELAND 6, WALES 3

After beating France 13–6 in Paris, England 11–10 at Twickenham and the Scots 6–0 at Lansdowne Road, on 13 March 1948 Ireland faced Wales at Ravenhill, Belfast, in their final game of the Five Nations Championship. Irish fans held their breath, knowing that a win over Wales would take their side to success they had never previously known. Ireland, thanks to their non-stop tackling and superior pace up front, won a tight game 6–3 to claim not only their first Triple Crown since 1899, but their first ever Grand Slam. The Welsh took the unwanted wooden spoon.

## ✌ RECORD TRY-SCORER IN A GAME ✌

The record for the highest number of tries in a championship match is held by Scotland's George Lindsay, who scored five tries in their 20–0 win over Wales in the 1887 Home Nations Championship. Scotland retained the title they won in 1886, while England propped up the table.

## ✌ THAT TRY! ✌

Gareth Edwards's try for the Barbarians against the All Blacks in January 1973 at Cardiff Arms Park is often referred to as "that try!" Many believe it was the greatest try ever scored, while Cliff Morgan's commentary of it conveys the drama of it: "Kirkpatrick to Williams. This is great stuff. Phil Bennett covering, chased by Alistair Scowan. Brilliant! Oh, that's brilliant! John Williams, Brian Williams, Pullin, John Dawes. Great dummy! David, Tom David, the half-way line. Brilliant by Quinnell. This is Gareth Edwards … a dramatic start … what a score! Oh, that fellow Edwards. If the greatest writer of the written word had written that story, no one would have believed it. That really was something." The Baa-Baas won 23–11, while six of the seven players involved in the try were Welsh – Phil Bennett, J. P. R. Williams, John Dawes, Tommy David, Derek Quinnell (father of Scott) and Edwards – sending the Cardiff Arms Park crowd into a frenzy of delight. "The game is one I will never forget and those of us who played in it will never be allowed to forget. It is a match that will live with me for ever. People tend only to remember the first four minutes of the game because of the try, but what they forget is the great deal of good rugby played afterwards, much of which came from the All Blacks," said Edwards.

# ✿ A HISTORIC GAME ✿

On 11 February 2007, Ireland played France at Croke Park (*Páirc an Chrócaigh*) in the Six Nations Championship. It was a historic occasion as it was the first time Ireland had been allowed to play a Rugby Union game at the sacred home of the Gaelic Athletic Association (GAA). The stadium was opened in 1913 and was traditionally used for Gaelic football and hurling. However, with Lansdowne Road under reconstruction the GAA permitted the Irish Rugby Union (IRU) to use Croke Park until their new home was ready. Ireland lost an epic encounter 20–17, and the French went on to win the Six Nations Championship with a points difference just four points better than Ireland's, although Ireland had the consolation of retaining their Triple Crown title, having beaten England, Scotland and Wales. Previously, throughout its colourful history, the GAA (*Cumann Lúthchleas Gael*), founded in 1884 as a nationalist organization, had always insisted on promoting indigenous Irish sport and believed that it was honour-bound to oppose other, foreign sports. Until the early 1970s, Rule 27 of the GAA constitution stated that a member of the GAA could be banned from playing its games if that member was found to be playing cricket, rugby or soccer. Even after Rule 27 was abolished, Rule 42 strictly prohibited the use of GAA property for games with interests in conflict with the interests of the GAA. At the GAA Annual Congress on 16 April 2005, a motion to temporarily relax Rule 42 was passed by 227 votes to 97 – 11 votes more than the required two-thirds majority. The GAA now had its members' authority to allow Ireland's international Rugby Union matches, as well as the Republic of Ireland football team's international matches, to be played at Croke Park until Lansdowne Road's redevelopment work was completed.

### *Did You Know That?*
Croke Park staged two American football games long before Rugby Union was permitted on the hallowed turf.

# ✿ PRIDE OF THE PACK ✿

When Martin Johnson, the Leicester Tigers and England lock forward, was named the captain of the British Lions for their 1997 tour of South Africa, he became only the third player at second-row forward to lead a Lions tour against the Springboks, following Willie John McBride in 1974 and Bill Beaumont in 1980. Johnson famously captained the Lions to a 2–1 win.

## ⚜ WIT AND WISDOM OF RUGBY (5) ⚜

"To score a try, one needs to engage in a series of actions that, in every other contest, could get a 15-year sentence to jail."
**P. G. Wodehouse**

## ⚜ COACH OF THE YEAR ⚜

The BBC Sports Personality of the Year Coach Award is voted for by the general public towards the end of the calendar year, and is presented to the coach/manager considered to have made the greatest contribution to sport from that year. It was first presented in 1999, when it was won by Sir Alex Ferguson. Clive Woodward, who received the award in 2003, the year of England's 2003 World Cup victory, is the only Rugby Union coach to have won it.

## ⚜ O'GARA OUT ON HIS OWN ⚜

Ireland's Ronan O'Gara holds the record for the most Championship appearances with a staggering 63 games for his country in the Six Nations (2000–13). O'Gara's compatriot Mike Gibson holds the Five Nations Championship record with 56 appearances, 1964–79.

## ⚜ JUDGED BY WINS ALONE ⚜

During the early years of the Home International Championship, which began back in 1883, there was no points system. Instead, teams were judged simply on whether they won or lost matches.

## ⚜ THEIR FIRST RENDEZVOUS ⚜

In March 1906, England met France for the first time in an international, the visitors (England) winning 35–8.

## ⚜ JIM RENWICK ⚜

Jim Renwick, one of Scotland's greatest ever players, won 52 caps for his country. He made his debut, aged 19, on 15 January 1972 in a 20–9 win over France at Murrayfield in the Five Nations Championship. When he retired from international rugby in 1984 he held Scotland's record for the highest number of appearances. Renwick was an attacking outside centre who possessed a quick turn of foot coupled with an ability to jink and weave his way past defenders.

# 🎵 ITALIAN RUGBY ANTHEM 🎵

**Il Canto degli Italiani** *(The Song of the Italians)*

Fratelli d'Italia,
L'Italia s'è desta,
Dell'elmo di Scipio
s'è cinta la testa.
Dov'è la Vittoria?
Le porga la chioma,
che schiava di Roma
Iddio la creò.

*CORO (Chorus)*
Stringiamoci a coorte,
siam pronti alla morte.
Siam pronti alla morte,
L'Italia chiamò.
Stringiamoci a coorte,
siam pronti alla morte.
Siam pronti alla morte,
L'Italia chiamò!

Noi fummo da secoli
calpesti, derisi,
perché non siam popolo,
perché siam divisi.
Raccolgaci un'unica
bandiera, una speme:
di fonderci insieme
già l'ora suonò.

*CORO*

Uniamoci, amiamoci,
L'unione e l'amore

rivelano ai popoli
le vie del Signore.
Giuriamo far libero
il suolo natio:
uniti, per Dio,
chi vincer ci può?

*CORO*

Dall'Alpi a Sicilia
Dovunque è Legnano,
Ogn'uom di Ferruccio
Ha il core, ha la mano,
I bimbi d'Italia
Si chiaman Balilla,
Il suon d'ogni squilla
I Vespri suonò.

*CORO*

Son giunchi che piegano
Le spade vendute:
Già l'Aquila d'Austria
Le penne ha perdute.
Il sangue d'Italia,
Il sangue Polacco,
Bevé, col cosacco,
Ma il cor le bruciò.

*CORO*

### Did You Know That?

The song was written in Genoa in the autumn of 1847 by a 20-year-old student, Goffredo Mameli, and put to music by Michele Novaro. The song was composed at a time when Italians were struggling for independence from Austria and for unification. It is often referred to as "Fratelli d'Italia" (Brothers of Italy).

## ✌ IF YOU KNOW YOUR HISTORY – 3 ✌

England won the inaugural Home International Championships in 1883 along with the Triple Crown.

## ✌ THE FFR ✌

The French Rugby Federation, or *Fédération française de rugby* (FFR), was formed in 1919 and is the governing body for Rugby Union throughout France. In 1978 the FFR became a member of the International Rugby Board (IRB).

## ✌ CAKED IN MUD ✌

On 5 February 1972 Gareth Edwards scored a try for Wales in their 35–12 hammering of Scotland at the National Stadium, Cardiff, in the Five Nations Championship which fans still talk about today. From a scrum deep in his own half, Edwards raced the length of the field to score a try in the corner. When he got up off the ground a photographer took the now famous and instantly recognizable photograph of Edwards caked in the red mud from the dog track that used to surround the Arms Park Stadium. Bill McLaren, commentating on the game for the BBC, described the try as follows: "It's beautifully laid back for Gareth Edwards, Edwards over the 25-yard line, over half-way, the kick ahead by Edwards, can he get there? It would be a miracle if he could. And he has!!! The sheer magic of Gareth Edwards has brought the whole of this stadium to its feet. You can see on his face the power, the strength, the fitness that took him there."

## ✌ FRENCH GRAND SLAM ✌

France won their first Grand Slam (it is *Le Grand Chelem* in French) in 1968 but they have added eight more since then. That said, France also endured a long wait for their first Five Nations Championship: it came in 1953 – 43 years and 24 tournaments after their debut.

## ✌ WELSH HAT-TRICK ✌

In 1911 Wales claimed their third Grand Slam title in what was only the second edition of the Five Nations Championship (but the 29th if including the Home Nations). No other country had won even one Grand Slam before Wales claimed their hat-trick of titles.

## ⚜ A CUB TURNED LION ⚜

Martin Corry played rugby for England at schools, college, Under-21 and "A" level before being awarded his first senior cap against Argentina in 1997. A versatile player who was comfortable at lock, blind-side or No. 8, he was very often used as a substitute, coming on when an impact was needed in the game. He played three Tests (winning one cap) for the British Lions on their 2001 tour of Australia (lost 2–1). He then played in the delayed final game of the 2001 Six Nations Championship in Dublin on 20 October 2001, which Ireland won 20–14 while England still secured the title, and was a bench replacement for the 2002 Six Nations. In 2003 he was part of England's World Cup side, and in 2005 he was named as the captain of England for their Six Nations Championship games against Italy and Scotland in the absence of Jason Robinson. Later that year he took part in his second Lions tour (lost 3–0 to New Zealand), having been appointed vice-captain. However, in the first Test he found himself leading the team when a spear tackle to Brian O'Driscoll forced the Ireland and Lions captain out of the game. In 2007 he was a member of the England side that reached the final of the Rugby World Cup, but prior to the start of the 2008 Six Nations Championship he announced his retirement from international rugby, aged 34.

## ⚜ WILL NOTCHES UP HIS HALF-CENTURY ⚜

On 6 March 2004, Will Greenwood won his 50th cap for England in their 19–13 loss to Ireland at Twickenham in the Six Nations Championship. He went on to win another five caps for his country playing against Australia in 2004. Will scored 31 tries for England. In 2005 he went on his third British Lions tour, to New Zealand, winning the first of his three Lions caps in the first Test when he replaced the injured Brian O'Driscoll, while the Lions lost the Test series 3–0.

## ⚜ LAYING THE FOUNDATION ⚜

With England (1907), Wales (1908) and Ireland (1909) all having played France in an international, the foundations for an annual Five Nations Championship were firmly laid in 1910 when the last of the home nations, Scotland, met the French in 1910. Scotland beat France 27–0 at Murrayfield on 22 January 1910 in what was the inaugural Five Nations Championship, won by England.

## ❧ CAPTAIN AND COACH OF THE *AZZURRI* ❧

Marco Bollesan made his debut for Italy in 1963 and went on to win 47 caps for the *Azzurri*, 37 of them as captain. He took charge of the Italian national team for three years from 1995, and from 2003–08 he was the Public Relations Officer for the Italian Rugby Federation.

## ❧ FRANCE LEAD THE WAY ❧

In the 14 years of the Six Nations Championship, 2000–13, each country has played 70 games. France and England have both won 47, Ireland 45, Wales 37, Scotland 18 and Italy 11. In terms of points, it is France 96, England 95, Ireland 92, Wales 76, Scotland 38 and Italy 23.

## ❧ GRACIOUS GARETH ❧

After being declared the greatest player of all time in a poll of international rugby players conducted in 2003 by *Rugby World* magazine, Gareth Edwards admitted that Sid Going, the famous All Blacks scrum-half, got the better of him over their seven encounters. "As I say, he was the best I played against and, yes, he probably had the edge on me in the games we played."

### *Did You Know That?*
When Edwards wrote his autobiography he was branded a "professional" and was prevented from coaching or being involved in any way with the sport of Rugby Union.

## ❧ HIGH FIVES FOR EDDIE ❧

When Ireland beat Scotland 40–13 at Murrayfield in the Six Nations Championship on 10 February 2005, it was the fifth straight win over the Scots for Irish national coach, Eddie O'Sullivan, since taking the Ireland job in 2002. March 2002: Ireland 43 Scotland 22 (Lansdowne Road); February 2003: Scotland 6 Ireland 36 (Murrayfield); September 2003: Scotland 10 Ireland 29 (Murrayfield); and March 2004: Ireland 37 Scotland 16 (Lansdowne Road). The win was also Ireland's sixth successive victory in the Six Nations Championship, while Scotland's head coach Matt Williams was still waiting for his first win in the tournament since taking over in 2004. Indeed, the Scots' loss meant that they had failed to record a tournament win since beating Italy 33–25 in March 2003 at Murrayfield.

## 🏉 JEAN-PIERRE RIVES – *LE CASQUE D'OR* 🏉

Jean-Pierre Rives was born on 31 December 1952 in Toulouse, in south-west France. Rugby mad in his youth, Rives played club rugby for TOEC, Beaumont and Stade Toulousain (his home-town club), and then in 1981 he left Toulouse and signed for Racing Club de Paris. Many French sports writers questioned whether someone of his height (5 ft 10 ins) could have a successful career playing as an open-side flanker, but Rives went on to become one of the greatest players of all time.

Jean-Pierre proudly played for his country at schools, junior, university and "B" international level before graduating to the senior French side. On 1 February 1975, he was awarded his first senior cap for France in a Five Nations game against England at Twickenham. The French had already lost 25–10 to Wales in Pars, but they were a different team with the mercurial Rives in the side, dashing around the pitch with verve and skill. France beat England 27–20 that day and Rives kept his place in the team as they lost only twice in his next 13 games for *Les Bleus*. The French public adored their new-found hero. Here was a player who possessed the sublime skill of a dashing three-quarter coupled with a rock-like presence at the back of a gigantic French forward pack. Moreover, despite his lack of inches Rives had the courage of a lion, the speed of a cheetah and the vision of a hawk. On many occasions his desire to win could be seen in the red streaks of blood flowing down his long blond locks following yet another confrontation on the pitch against someone almost twice his size. In his book, *100 Great Rugby Players*, the legendary Gareth Edwards said of Rives that "the sheer will to win and naked aggression of the super-charged flanker was enough to put opposing players off their stride".

In 1977 he helped France to the Grand Slam title, and the following year he succeeded Bastiat as French captain. He captained France to the Grand Slam in 1981 and led them to their first win over the All Blacks in 1979. Between 1975 and 1984 Rives won 59 caps for France, a record for a flanker, and is France's most capped captain with 34 caps. In 1977, 1979 and 1981 he was named France's player of the year. Without question Rives, nicknamed *Casque d'Or* (Golden Helmet), was one of France's most charismatic leaders, while his Gallic flair was evident in his tactical awareness, his distribution skills, his courage in defence and his cavalier attacking play.

In retirement, Rives turned his attention to art, and he became an internationally renowned sculptor based in Paris.

### Did You Know That?
Another of Jean-Pierre Rives's nicknames was "Asterix" (from the French comic strip), because of his blond hair and bravery.

## ✌ MOST APPEARANCES IN FIVE/SIX NATIONS ✌

These players have appeared at least 50 times in the Five/Six Nations:

| Caps | | Player | Country | Career |
|------|---|--------|---------|--------|
| 63 | ❖ | Ronan O'Gara | Ireland | 2000–2012 |
| 60 | ❖ | Brian O'Driscoll | Ireland | 2000–2013 |
| 56 | ❖ | Mike Gibson | Ireland | 1964–1979 |
| 54 | ❖ | John Hayes | Ireland | 2000–2010 |
| 54 | ❖ | Jason Leonard | England | 1991–2004 |
| 53 | ❖ | Willie John McBride | Ireland | 1962–1975 |
| 53 | ❖ | Chris Paterson | Scotland | 2000–2011 |
| 51 | ❖ | Martyn Williams | Wales | 1998–2010 |
| 50 | ❖ | Stephen Jones | Wales | 2000–2011 |
| 50 | ❖ | Philippe Sella | France | 1983–1995 |
| 50 | ❖ | Rory Underwood | England | 1984–1996 |

## ✌ THE FLYING DRAGON ✌

Nigel Walker won 17 caps (scoring 12 tries) for Wales as a winger in the mid-1990s, but prior to winning his first cap against Ireland on 6 March 1993 Walker was better known for his achievements in athletics than rugby. He was a member of the Great Britain athletics team at the 1984 Olympic Games in Los Angeles, and competed in the 110m hurdles (Roger Kingdom from the USA won the gold medal).

## ✌ WHEN FIVE BECAME SIX ✌

When French winger Philippe Bernat-Salles scored a try in each of his team's 2001 Six Nations Championship matches, he became only the sixth player in the history of the competition to complete this landmark achievement and the first to do so in the expanded format. The others were H. C. Catcheside (England, 1924), A. C. Wallace (Scotland, 1925), Patrick Estève (France, 1983), Philippe Sella (France, 1986) and Gregor Townsend (Scotland, 1999).

## ✌ SWAPPING THEIR BALLS ✌

Three Gaelic footballers successfully switched codes to Rugby Union and went on to play for Ireland: David Beggy (Meath County Team), who played Rugby Union for Leinster; Mick Galwey (Kerry County Team), who played Rugby Union for Munster, and Brian Rigney (Offaly County Team), who played Rugby Union for Leinster.

# ❧ GRAND SLAMS (3) – SCOTLAND 1925 ❧

Scottish rugby opened their new home in 1925, Murrayfield Stadium in Edinburgh. And they gave it a magnificent baptism by claiming a first ever Grand Slam. Scotland, who had seen off France, Wales and Ireland, had a chance of winning the Slam while 15 March visitors England – who had drawn 6–6 with Ireland – had hopes of a third consecutive title. A pulsating match saw the lead change hands three times in the second half before Scotland prevailed 14–11 with a Herbert Waddell drop goal.

### FIVE NATIONS CHAMPIONSHIP 1925

| Team | P | W | D | L | PF | PA | Pts |
|---|---|---|---|---|---|---|---|
| Scotland | 4 | 4 | 0 | 0 | 77 | 37 | 8 |
| Ireland | 4 | 2 | 1 | 1 | 42 | 26 | 5 |
| England | 4 | 2 | 1 | 1 | 42 | 37 | 5 |
| Wales | 4 | 1 | 0 | 3 | 34 | 60 | 2 |
| France | 4 | 0 | 0 | 4 | 23 | 58 | 0 |

### RESULTS 1925

| Date | Venue | Opponent | Score | Captains |
|---|---|---|---|---|
| 24 January | Edinburgh | France | 25–4 | GPS Macpherson |
| 7 February | Swansea | Wales | 24–14 | GPS Macpherson |
| 28 February | Dublin | Ireland | 14–8 | GPS Macpherson |
| 15 March | Edinburgh | England | 14–11 | GPS Macpherson |

*Did You Know That?*
Ian Smith, George Aitken, Johnny Wallace and Phil Macpherson, the Scottish three-quarter line, were all students at Oxford University, but they never played together for the Dark Blues.

# ❧ THE MURPHY SEVENS ❧

Ireland's Geordan Edward Andrew Murphy was actually named George when he was born, after his father, but his mother decided to call him Geordan to avoid any confusion. His six brothers and sister all played Rugby Union. He was awarded his first Irish cap on 10 June 2000 in Ireland's 83–3 win over the USA in New Hampshire, USA. In 2005 he was capped by the British Lions on their tour of New Zealand. Up until the departure of Eddie O'Sullivan as the Irish coach on 19 March 2008, Murphy had been overlooked for a place in the side in favour of Girvan Dempsey, who was O'Sullivan's first choice at full-back.

## ℘ WIT AND WISDOM OF RUGBY (6) ℘

"Have fun, work hard, have hobbies, play lots of different sports and be good to your mum!"
*Scott Murray on the secret of success*

## ℘ ANDY'S WORLD ℘

Andy Irvine's tally of 273 points for Scotland and a further 28 for the British Lions stood as a world record for five years after his international retirement, until it was broken by Australia's Michael Lynagh in 1987.

## ℘ LEADER OF THE BACKS ℘

During an interview which appeared in *The Sunday Times* on 25 March 2007, the legendary Welsh international, Cliff Morgan, was asked his opinion of his fellow countryman, Gareth Edwards. Morgan smiled, leant forward in his armchair and said: "The greatest rugby player ever born, in any position, anywhere in the world."

*Did You Know That?*
Edwards's 53 consecutive appearances from 1967 to 1978 constitute a national team record.

## ℘ IRISH LEADERS ℘

The IRFU first decided to appoint a coach in 1971, placing Ronnie Dawson in the hot seat. Here is a full list of those who have held the post:

Ronnie Dawson 1971–75
Roly Meates 1975–77
Noel Murphy 1977–80
Willie John McBride 1980–84
Mick Doyle 1984–87
Jim Davidson 1987–90
Ciaran Fitzgerald 1990–92
Gerry Murphy 1993–95
Murray Kidd 1995–97
Brian Ashton 1997–98
Warren Gatland 1998–2001
Eddie O'Sullivan 2001–08
Declan Kidney 2008–13

## ≈ 57 OLD FARTS ≈

In May 1995, during an interview for a Channel 4 documentary entitled *Fair Game*, the England captain Will Carling infamously described the members of the Rugby Football Union's committee as "57 old farts". His comments caused outrage among the sport's ruling body in England and resulted in a power struggle that was ultimately to determine the balance of power in the English game and herald the advent of professionalism in the sport. In reply to Carling's famous line the RFU secretary, Dudley Wood, commented: "Some of the committee may want to stand on their dignity ... It does not tell us much about the committee but it does tell us something about Will Carling." A few days after Carling's outburst was made public the RFU, widely known by this time as "the old farts", huddled together and conspired to have the young upstart Carling stripped of the England captaincy for the 1995 Rugby World Cup, which was due to commence the following month. They issued a statement that read: "It has been decided with regret that Will Carling's captaincy of the England team will be terminated forthwith and an announcement concerning his replacement will be made shortly. In the light of the view recently expressed regarding administrators, it is considered inappropriate for him to continue to represent, as England captain, the RFU, England and, indeed, English sport." However, much to the dismay of the old farts, when they approached senior England players to take over the captaincy from Carling, they were rebuffed. Two days after the first RFU statement, they released another which read: "Will Carling wishes to apologize to every member of the Committee for his inappropriate and gratuitously offensive comments at the end of a recent television programme. All 25 members of the England squad have indicated their support for Will Carling as captain and have respectfully requested the RFU officers to reconsider their decision to terminate the appointment. Will Carling would like to thank the squad for their support and also Denis Easby for his courage in reconsidering the original decision, thus enabling the England squad to have a settled and successful build-up to the World Cup. In light of these circumstances, the RFU are agreeable to reinstating Will Carling as England's captain for the period of the World Cup."

## ≈ HISTORY REVISITED ≈

Wales's 2008 RBS Six Nations Championship win and Grand Slam came exactly 100 years after their first.

## ❧ EPIC GAMES (4) ☙

### 1951 – ENGLAND 3, FRANCE 11

On 24 February 1951, France recorded their first ever success at Twickenham, an 11–3 win in the Five Nations Championship. The man of the match was the French captain Jean Prat, who scored eight of his nation's points with a try, a conversion and a drop goal. However, it would be a further eight years before France claimed their inaugural Five Nations Championship crown.

## ❧ LUCKY 13 FOR WALES ☙

In 1953 Wales won their fifth Grand Slam, the 13th time a country had won all of their games in a Home or Five Nations Championship.

## ❧ ENGLAND'S BRICKIE ☙

Prior to becoming a full-time Rugby Union player, future England centre Jeremy Guscott was a bricklayer. He scored a hat-trick of tries on his England debut, a 58–3 win over Romania in Bucharest on 13 May 1989. Jeremy went on to win 65 caps for his country, scoring 143 points, and played for the British Lions 23 times (1989, 1993 and 1997, winning 8 caps and scoring 41 points). Guscott made his final international appearance on 15 October 1999 versus Tonga in a World Cup pool match at Twickenham (England won 101–10). He was coolness personified on the field.

## ❧ FOR CLUB AND COUNTRY ☙

Pierre Berbizier played 56 times for France, mainly at scrum-half. He made his debut on 17 January 1981 in their 16–9 win over Scotland in Paris in a Five Nations Championship game. In 1987 he captained the French to Grand Slam glory, and he won his last cap for France on 16 March 1991 in their Five Nations Championship 21–19 defeat at Twickenham. In 1992 he was appointed the head coach of the French national team and guided *Les Bleus* to the semi-finals of the 1995 Rugby World Cup before being sacked in 1995 after he fell out with the president of the French Rugby Federation, Bernard Lapasset. In 2005 he was appointed head coach of Italy.

*Did You Know That?*
Under Berbizier, in 2007, Italy won two matches in a single Six Nations Championship tournament for the first time.

## THE TRIPLE CROWN TROPHY

The Triple Crown trophy is a silver dish measuring 42 cm wide and 5 cm deep and weighing 3 kg. Despite the long and illustrious history of the Triple Crown a permanent trophy did not exist for the winning nation until 2006, when the primary sponsor of the Six Nations competition, the Royal Bank of Scotland, commissioned a trophy to be awarded to the Triple Crown winners. The Triple Crown trophy was first competed for in the 2007 RBS Six Nations and was won by Ireland. A last-minute try from Ireland's Shane Horgan against England at Twickenham on 18 March 2007 gave the Irish a 56–28 victory, and Brian O'Driscoll became the first man to lift the Triple Crown trophy. The Triple Crown trophy is housed in the Museum of Rugby at Twickenham.

## ROGER AND OUT

Roger Miles Uttley won 23 caps for England, playing in both the back row and second row, five times as captain. On 10 February 1973, Uttley made his debut in an 18–9 defeat to Ireland at Lansdowne Road in the Five Nations Championship (England won the wooden spoon in 1973). He played in four Tests during the British Lions' undefeated tour to South Africa in 1974 (won 3–0). Roger was also assistant coach to the 1989 British Lions side that won their Test series 2–1 against Australia. Roger is an honorary member of the rugby charity Wooden Spoon, which helps disadvantaged children and young people in Britain and Ireland.

## WHEN THE TEACHER ENDED THE CLASS

During an interview with Paul Kimmage which appeared in *The Sunday Times* on 25 March 2007, the legendary Welsh international Gareth Edwards was reminded of the day he decided that he did not want to become a teacher. "Teaching practice was the start of it, just being among the kids and realizing, 'God! Can I do this? How am I going to cope?' The thought of doing it for the rest of my life did not turn me on, and it was highlighted for me by the vice-principal of the college, Eric Thomas, a beautifully dressed, articulate man who loved the students and his job. One day he gave us this informal lecture: 'Gentlemen,' he said, 'your rewards from teaching won't be monetary, they will come from your inner self. Love it, and it will give you great satisfaction, but if you don't, get out, because it will only destroy you.' It was a huge release and burden off my shoulders. I got out."

## ✷ WINNERS ARE ACTUALLY LOSERS ✷

Going into their final match of the 2008 RBS Six Nations Championship, against Italy at the Stadio Flaminio in Rome, Scotland's players knew that losing to the Italians by five points or more would leave them with the wooden spoon for the second consecutive season. Scotland were indeed beaten, but the final score was 23–20 and this meant it was their hosts who ended up with the wooden spoon.

## ✷ BILLY TWELVETREES ✷

Billy Twelvetrees made his debut for England in the 2013 Six Nations, scoring a try in the 38–18 defeat of Scotland at Twickenham. Before the game, the origin of his surname attracted attention. Billy's grandfather, 88-year-old Walter, explained that it lies with Billy's mother, Beverley. She was the last of his three daughters to marry and his two other daughters had already taken their husbands' surnames. Beverley wanted to keep her surname and asked her fiancé, Kevin Fentiman, to change his surname. Kevin – a tree surgeon – willingly agreed

## ✷ WITH BALL IN HAND AND AT FEET ✷

Tony Ward won 19 caps at fly-half for Ireland between 1978 and 1987, scoring 113 points (29 penalties, 7 conversions and 4 drop goals). He made his Irish debut on 21 January 1978, in a 12–9 win over Scotland at Lansdowne Road, Dublin, in the Five Nations Championship. He scored a total of 38 points in the 1978 championship, a record for a debutant at the time. Later that year, on 31 October, Ward inspired Munster to a legendary 12–0 victory against the All Blacks at Thomond Park, scoring two drop goals and a conversion. Munster remain the only Irish team ever to beat New Zealand. Tony made his final Irish appearance on 3 June 1987 at the Rugby World Cup finals, a 32–9 win over Tonga in Brisbane, Australia. Tony also won one cap for the British Lions, during their tour of South Africa in 1980, and set a Lions Test record by scoring 18 points, including five penalties and a drop goal. His achievement was also a record for any player against the Springboks.

### *Did You Know That?*
Tony was also a gifted association footballer. He played for Shamrock Rovers and Limerick United, helping the latter to FAI Cup glory in 1982.

# ❧ FANTASY TEAMS – SCOTLAND XV ❧

**1** David **SOLE** *(capt)*
**2** Colin **DEANS**
**3** Iain **MILNE**
**4** Gordon **BROWN**
**5** Scott **MURRAY**
**6** John **JEFFREY**
**7** Finlay **CALDER**
**8** Simon **TAYLOR**
**9** Gary **ARMSTRONG**
**10** John **RUTHERFORD**
**11** Roger **BAIRD**
**12** Jim **RENWICK**
**13** Alan **TAIT**
**14** Andy **IRVINE**
**15** Gavin **HASTINGS**

*Replacements*
16 Kenny *LOGAN* ❖ 17 Scott *HASTINGS* ❖ 18 Dodie *WEIR*
19 Jim *CALDER* ❖ 20 Sandy *CARMICHAEL* ❖ 21 Ian M*ACLOUGHLIN*
22 Gordon *BULLOCH* ❖ 23 Richie *GRAY*
*Coach*
Sir Ian *McGEECHAN*

## *Did You Know That?*

Sir Ian McGeechan was a coach when Scotland won the Five Nations Grand Slam in 1990 and was the British Lions coach on their tours of 1989, 1993 and 1997. He led the Lions tour of South Africa in 2009, the same year he received a knighthood for his services to rugby.

## ❧ BLOWN AWAY ❧

Despite winning two Grand Slams with the French in 1981 and 1987, Serge Blanco's one big regret from his playing career was that he was never able to win the French national championship with his club side, Biarritz Olympique, whom he loyally served from 1974 to 1992. During his career Blanco was generally regarded as a fitness fanatic, even though it was claimed that he smoked up to 75 cigarettes a day. His smoking certainly did not affect his blistering speed – he smoked defenders all over the world with his great power and pace.

## ❧ FROM INVERLEITH TO MURRAYFIELD ❧

The last ever international match to be played at Inverleith, Edinburgh, took place on 25 January 1925 (Burns' Day), when Scotland beat France 25–4. Murrayfield was officially opened on 21 March 1925 with England, the reigning Five Nations Champions, providing the opposition. A partisan crowd of 70,000 cheered their Scottish heroes on to a memorable 14–11 win over their bitter rivals to claim Scotland's first ever Grand Slam title. The War Memorial Arch, which had been erected at Inverleith in 1921, was transferred to Murrayfield in 1936.

## ❧ ENGLISH CAPTAIN SNUBS IRISH PRESIDENT ❧

On 30 March 2003, the England captain Martin Johnson broke official protocol when he refused to stand in front of the red carpet parade area prior to England's Six Nations Championship game against Ireland at Lansdowne Road, Dublin. Johnson's actions led to the Irish president, Mary McAleese, having to walk across the uncovered grass to greet him and his team-mates. The match itself was a winner-takes-all Grand Slam decider which the visitors won 42–16. The media made a huge issue of Johnson's snub of the Irish president, but he refused to apologize for his actions.

## ❧ THE LEGEND BEGINS ❧

When Gareth Edwards arrived at Millfield School, in Somerset, his PE teacher was Bill Samuels. "What position do you want to play?" Samuels asked him. "Centre," replied the young Edwards. "Forget it – look at the size of you!" Samuel exclaimed. "You'll make a scrum-half." Edwards was quick to agree. "OK," he said. "What do I have to do?"

## ❧ THE FRENCH SEX SYMBOL ❧

France's Christophe Dominici scored on his debut against England on 7 February 1998 in their 24–17 win in the Five Nations Championship at the Stade de France. Dominici went on to win 65 caps for his country and retired after France's defeat to Argentina in the third-place play-off game at the 2007 Rugby World Cup. In 2006, after Dominici appeared in the *Dieux du Stade* (*Gods of the Stadium*) calendar, he became extremely popular among the gay community, who regard him as a sex symbol.

## ❧ FAMOUS VARSITY PLAYERS ❧

A number of players who have played in the annual Varsity Match between Cambridge University and Oxford University have gone on to win international honours for their respective nations, including:

Stuart Barnes (Oxford)
Simon Danielli (Oxford)
David Humphreys (Oxford)
Rob Andrew (Cambridge)
Phil de Glanville (Oxford)
Nick Mallett (Oxford)
Gareth Rees (Oxford)
Simon Amor (Cambridge)
Mike Gibson (Cambridge)
Gavin Hastings (Cambridge)

## ❧ YOUNGEST DRAGON TO 50 CAPS ❧

David Peel became the youngest player to win 50 caps for Wales when he played in their 21–9 defeat by Scotland at Murrayfield in the RBS Six Nations Championship. He was 25 years old at the time and was the 17th Welsh international to reach the half-century mark. Amazingly, Peel won his 50th cap in just six years, whereas the first Welsh player to achieve the feat, the legendary Gareth Edwards, took nearly 11 years to win his 50.

## ❧ THE ITALIAN HOOKER ❧

Alessandro Moscardi was an Italian hooker who played in 45 internationals for his country, including 17 as captain. He made his debut against Portugal in 1993 and played his last game for the *Azzurri* in the 2002 Six Nations Championship, when Italy lost 45–9 to England at the Stadio Flaminio, Rome. Moscardi led Treviso to the Italian title before announcing his retirement from club rugby in the summer of 2003.

## ❧ IF YOU KNOW YOUR HISTORY – 4 ❧

From 1883, the first year of the Home Nations Championship, until 1892 England and Scotland were the only winners. Wales captured their first title in 1893. Ireland won their first Home Nations title in 1894, the last of the four to claim a championship crown.

## ℘ WIT AND WISDOM OF RUGBY (7) ℘

"The lads say my bum is the equivalent of one Erica."
*Bill Beaumont*

## ℘ SEVENTH HEAVEN FOR ENGLAND ℘

In 1967 England claimed their seventh Grand Slam title in what was the 28th edition of the Five Nations Championship and the 63rd involving the original four home nations. Wales now trailed England by four Grand Slams.

## ℘ IN THE DRAGON'S DEN ℘

In 1967 David Nash was appointed as the Welsh national team's first coach following their unsuccessful tour to South Africa in 1964. After the appointment of nine consecutive Welsh-born coaches, the Welsh Rugby Union opted for a foreign influence in 1995, bringing in Alex Evans from Australia. In 2007 New Zealander Warren Gatland became the principality's 20th coach, and up until the end of May 2008 had not lost a game in charge, guiding the Welsh to the Six Nations Championship Grand Slam in 2008.

## ℘ D'ARCY MY BOY ℘

Gordon William D'Arcy made his international debut for Ireland on 15 October 1999 as a replacement against Romania during the 1999 Rugby World Cup finals, Ireland winning 44–14. However, he did not pull on the Irish jersey again until 17 November 2002 (coming on as a replacement in their 64–17 win over Fiji), having been omitted from the Irish set-up following a fall-out with his Provincial coaches concerning his attitude. His career took a topsy-turvy shape over the next few years – he was left out of Ireland's 2003 Rugby World Cup squad – before he finally established his place in the team, ironically as a direct result of an injury to his Leinster team-mate, Brian O'Driscoll, which allowed D'Arcy a good run in the side. In 2004 he was named the Six Nations Player of the Tournament and helped the Irish to their first Triple Crown since 1985. With O'Driscoll fit again, Ireland now had a centre partnership second to none. D'Arcy toured New Zealand with the British Lions in 2005 and played in all of Ireland's Six Nations Championship games in 2006 and 2007, winning the RBS Six Nations Player of the Tournament award in 2007.

*O*

## ❧ BILL McLAREN – THE VOICE OF RUGBY ❧

Bill McLaren was born in Hawick, Scotland, in 1923 and was a talented flanker in his day. Prior to World War 2 he broke into the Hawick XV, and in 1947 he was offered a run-out in a Scotland trial. However, he contracted tuberculosis while serving with the army in Italy during the war, which ended his dreams of pulling on the famous blue jersey of his country. Some 19 months later, after lengthy treatment for TB, he performed his first commentary during his convalescence, describing table tennis games for the hospital's radio station. McLaren then studied physical education in Aberdeen before going on to forge a career as a PE instructor which lasted until 1987. Combining his PE duties with a stint as a reporter for the *Hawick Express*, he made his national commentary debut for BBC radio on 7 February 1953. It was a bittersweet debut as Scotland lost 12–0 to Wales at Murrayfield. Six years later McLaren switched to the screen and BBC television.

In November 2001, the International Rugby Hall of Fame paid the ultimate tribute to McLaren when they made him the first non-international to be inducted. After 50 years of commentating, during which time he became known as "the voice of rugby", McLaren retired. Fittingly, his final commentary was Scotland's 27–22 Six Nations Championship defeat of Wales in Cardiff on 6 April 2002. Prior to the kick-off McLaren was acknowledged by Scottish and Welsh fans alike when a packed Millennium Stadium rocked with a rousing rendition of "For He's a Jolly Good Fellow". Following the Scots' victory the Welsh legend Jonathan Davies paid a personal tribute to McLaren in which he said: "The respect people have for Bill is amazing. On behalf of everyone in rugby, thanks. You will leave behind a huge void." A tearful McLaren simply said: "It will be a terrible wrench to leave, but my wife Bette has a little list of jobs for me to do. I have had a great time but I am ready to put my feet up now. I just wish I could have won that one cap."

McLaren's most memorable sporting moments include watching his son-in-law, Alan Lawson, score two tries for Scotland against England in 1976 in their 22–12 win in a Five Nations game, and Scotland beating England to clinch the Grand Slam title in 1990. McLaren provided many memorable quotes behind a BBC microphone, but perhaps his most famous quip of all was, "Aye, they'll be dancing in the streets of Hawick tonight." Bill McLaren died on 10 January 2010, aged 86.

### Did You Know That?

As a PE instructor McLaren coached several players who went on to play for Scotland, including Alister Campbell, Colin Deans, Jim Renwick and Tony Stanger.

# ❧ PHILIPPE SELLA – SIMPLY *MAGNIFIQUE* ❧

Philippe Sella was born on 14 February 1962 in Tonneins, south-west France. Other than Bastille Day he could not have been born on a more appropriate date than Valentine's Day, given the love the French people had for their most capped player. From 1982 to 1995 he played for Agen, joining Saracens in 1996. On 31 October 1982, he made his international debut for *Les Bleus* on the wing against Romania in a 13–9 loss in Bucharest. A month later he had two superb games against Argentina ahead of the 1983 Five Nations Championship (France won 25–12 in Toulouse and 13–6 in Paris). From the moment he pulled on the French shirt everyone could see he was a very special player in the making. Six of his first seven internationals were on the wing, jinking and weaving his way past defenders. After moving to inside centre, he continued his magic, scoring tries for fun along the way.

In 1983 he played in all four of France's Five Nations games, helping them to the title. Sella was the dynamic midfield linchpin for France, Five Nations runners-up to Scotland in 1984 (scoring three tries), runners-up to Ireland in 1985, winners in 1986, when he became one of the few players to score a try in every game of a Five Nations campaign – and in 1987 the French completed the Grand Slam. Of course no one player can win games on his own, but one player like Sella can inspire others around him to greatness. He would be the first to acknowledge the contribution of his partners in the engine room of the French midfield, rugby legends in their own right such as his first partner Didier Codorniou, then Denis Charvet, Marc Andrieu, Franck Mesnel and Thierry Lacroix. However, few would argue, least of all his partners, that whereas Serge Blanco (France 1980–91) probably grabbed all of the headlines for his explosive pace and try-scoring exploits in the French side of the 1980s, it was Sella who made the French tick. Sella quite simply had it all, including speed, strength, classic passing skills, a penetrative running style and a water-tight defence. Indeed, during the 1980s France won or shared the Five Nations Championship five times, with the dynamic Sella the focal point of their side at centre.

He played his last game for France on 22 June 1995, helping *Les Bleus* to a 19–9 win over England to claim third place at the 1995 Rugby World Cup finals in South Africa. When he retired, aged 36, he was the world's most capped player, with 111 (scoring 125 points). Without question Sella's magnificent array of skills made him the best centre of his generation.

## *Did You Know That?*
Sella helped Saracens to Tetley's Bitter Cup glory in 1998.

## ✦ 63 TRIPLE CROWNS ✦

Including the 2013 season, the Triple Crown (victories against the three other home nations) has been achieved 63 times: England has 23 wins, Wales 20, and Scotland and Ireland both 10. The most recent winners were Wales in 2012.

## ✦ SCOTLAND'S SOLE MAN ✦

David Sole won 44 caps as prop for Scotland between 1986 and 1992, with a record 25 of those appearances as captain, and scored 12 points for his country. David made his debut at Murrayfield against France on 18 January 1986 in the Scots' 18–17 Five Nations win. In 1989 he won three British Lions caps on their victorious tour of Australia and showed his outstanding leadership qualities by captaining the Lions on two occasions, acting as deputy to his national team-mate, Finlay Calder. The following year he led Scotland out at Murrayfield on 17 August 1990 for the Five Nations decider against England. Scotland won the game 13–7 to claim their third Grand Slam (after those of 1925 and 1984). Sole was an unmistakable character on the field with his white headband, but it was his superb ball-handling skills and ferocious tackling that set him apart from his peers. He also captained the Barbarians on a number of occasions, and in 1992 he enjoyed a memorable win over New Zealand as captain of a World Invitation XV. Sole's final game for Scotland was on 21 June 1992 in a 37–13 defeat by Australia in Brisbane.

## ✦ LAST ENGLISH DUAL INTERNATIONAL ✦

John W. Sutcliffe began his rugby career with Bradford in 1886 before joining Heckmondwike, where he won his only international cap for England against the New Zealand Natives in 1889. When the RFU suspended the Yorkshire club over allegations of professionalism among their ranks, Sutcliffe switched codes to association football and signed for Bolton Wanderers. In 1893, while at Bolton Wanderers, he won the first of his five England football caps (a 6–0 win over Wales), and after a brief spell with Millwall Athletic in 1902 he signed for Manchester United in 1903. He is the last player to win international caps for England in both sports.

*Did You Know That?*
Sutcliffe won an FA Cup runners-up medal with Bolton Wanderers in 1894.

## ❧ IF YOU KNOW YOUR HISTORY – 5 ❧

In 1908 and 1909 the Home International Championships were won by Wales, and the Principality could also lay claim to winning the Grand Slam in each of those years as they also beat France.

## ❧ A CLOSELY FOUGHT AFFAIR ❧

The 2007 RBS Six Nations Championship was very close. Four nations headed into the last round of games with a mathematical chance of being crowned champions. In the end France won on points difference.

## ❧ A SQUEAKY LION ❧

Rob Andrew, the former England international, was nicknamed "Squeaky". He won the first of his 70 England caps (two as captain) in a win over Romania in January 1985 at Twickenham, and over the next ten years established himself as a regular in the team. He scored a career total 396 international points, which places him third in the all-time list (behind Jonny Wilkinson and Paul Grayson), won three Grand Slam titles and holds the English record for the most points scored in an international, 30 against Canada in 1994.

## ❧ THE ITALIAN KIWI ❧

Rima Wakarua was born in Auckland, New Zealand, but plays international rugby for his adopted nation, Italy. Fly-half Wakarua is a naturalized Italian, having moved to Italy in 1999 with his New Zealand-born father and Scottish mother.

## ❧ A VERY ENGLISH AFFAIR ❧

Fernand Cazenave played six times for France as a winger in the 1950s. He made his debut against England on 25 February 1950 and scored his only try for his country in their 6–3 Five Nations Championship win in Colombes. He also played his last game for France against England, France winning 11–3 in Paris on 10 April 1954, again in the Five Nations Championship. After retiring as a player he took up coaching and guided Mont-de-Marsan to victory in the French Championship in 1963, the only time the club has ever won the title. In 1968 he succeeded former French team-mate Jean Prat as the coach of the French national side and remained in the post until 1973.

## ⚜ IN THE COURT OF SIR CLIVE ⚜

Sir Clive Woodward was in charge of the England national team for seven years from November 1997 until Andy Robinson took charge in October 2004. In total he was in charge for 83 games, the first a 15–15 draw with Australia at Twickenham, the last a 51–15 defeat by the Wallabies at the Suncorp Stadium, Brisbane. However, despite these two disappointing results England fared exceptionally well under his leadership, winning 71.1 per cent of their games in all competitions.

*Did You Know That?*
Jack Rowell, England manager from June 1994 to July 1997, when Clive Woodward succeeded him, holds the most impressive win percentage as England manager, with 72.4 per cent (P29, W21, D0, L8).

## ⚜ A VERY SPECIAL PUPIL ⚜

"I've got a boy here who could be very special." These are the immortal words written by Bill Samuels, the PE teacher at Millfield School, in Somerset, in a letter to Cardiff Rugby Club about his pupil, Gareth Edwards.

*Did You Know That?*
Samuels wrote his letter of application on blue paper with black ink (the Cardiff colours are black and blue).

## ⚜ A HISTORIC GAME ⚜

Many sportswriters consider England's William Wavell Wakefield (31 caps, 13 as captain, 18 points) as the greatest forward of the 1920s. He was clearly an automatic choice for the historic Centenary Match at Rugby School in 1923, when England and Wales played Scotland and Ireland for the first time.

## ⚜ AN ENGLISHMAN IN IRELAND ⚜

Brian Ashton coached the Irish national team from 18 January 1997 to 6 March 1998, and of his eight games in charge the Irish won only two and lost the other six. Ashton had originally been handed a six-year contract by the IRFU, but following his team's poor results he resigned after just 14 months.

## ❧ EPIC GAMES (5) ❧

### 1965 – ENGLAND 3, SCOTLAND 3

On 20 March 1965, England faced Scotland at Twickenham in each nation's last game of the 1965 Five Nations Championship. It was a battle to avoid the wooden spoon, as England had just one win under their belt (a 9–6 victory over France) in the tournament while the Scots had lost all three of their games. With just a few seconds left on the game clock the Scots led 3–0 and were poised to claim their first away win over their old enemy since 1938 (a 21–16 victory) before England's left wing, A. W. Hancock, scored one of the most dramatic tries ever seen at Twickenham to claim an unlikely draw for the home side and send Scotland to the bottom of the table. Hancock collected a pass and ran 85 yards down the left wing to score a try in the corner. France meanwhile denied Wales a Grand Slam title by beating the Welsh 22–13 in their final game in Paris.

## ❧ TRIPLE CROWN BUT NO GRAND SLAM ❧

In 2004 Ireland won the Triple Crown, but France won the Grand Slam. In 2007 Ireland won the Triple Crown again, but France won the Six Nations Championship.

## ❧ HALF-TON UP ❧

On 4 February 1978, Wales beat England 9–6 at Twickenham *en route* to winning the Grand Slam. In the game Gareth Edwards became the first Welsh player to notch up 50 caps for his country, having made his debut against France in Paris on 1 April 1967, also in the Five Nations Championship. It was his 50th consecutive game for his country and proved to be his last season of international rugby, in which he won his third Grand Slam at the age of 30.

***Did You Know That?***
The only other player in the history of international rugby who has won his first 50 caps in successive matches is Christian Cullen, for the All Blacks from 1996 to 2000.

## ❧ IT'S NOT JUST MEN ONLY ❧

Running alongside the Six Nations Championship are editions for men's Under-20s and women. In 2013, England were Under-20s champions for a third straight year and Ireland's women completed the Grand Slam.

# ❧ GRAND SLAMS (4) – IRELAND 1948 ❧

Until 2009, the only time Ireland celebrated winning a Grand Slam had been in 1948. They opened with a New Year's Day win in Paris, 13–6. Six weeks later they squeezed out a one-point win against England at Twickenham and then blanked Scotland 6–0 at Lansdowne Road. Before the 13 March game against Wales at Ravenhill, Belfast, captain Karl Mullen told his team, "If we play our best, we will win." Ulster fly-half Jackie Kyle was in top form and he orchestrated the 6–3 victory, secured with a try from lock John Daly.

### FIVE NATIONS CHAMPIONSHIP 1948

| Team | P | W | D | L | PF | PA | Pts |
|---|---|---|---|---|---|---|---|
| Ireland | 4 | 4 | 0 | 0 | 36 | 19 | 8 |
| France | 4 | 2 | 0 | 2 | 40 | 25 | 4 |
| Scotland | 4 | 2 | 0 | 2 | 15 | 31 | 4 |
| Wales | 4 | 1 | 1 | 2 | 23 | 20 | 3 |
| England | 4 | 0 | 1 | 4 | 16 | 35 | 1 |

### RESULTS 1948

| Date | Venue | Opponent | Score | Captains |
|---|---|---|---|---|
| 1 January | Paris | France | 13–6 | K Mullen |
| 14 February | Twickenham | England | 11–10 | K Mullen |
| 28 February | Dublin | Scotland | 6–0 | K Mullen |
| 13 March | Belfast | Wales | 6–3 | K Mullen |

*Did You Know That?*
On 30 March 2003, Ireland met England at Lansdowne Road, Dublin, with the Grand Slam at stake for the winners. There was no fairy tale for the Irish as England romped to a 42–6 triumph.

# ❧ IN BOD WE TRUST ❧

Ireland's Brian O'Driscoll has been voted the RBS Six Nations Championship Player of the Tournament three times, 2006, 2007 and 2009 (he captained Ireland to Grand Slam glory in 2009). He made his international debut for Ireland on 12 June 1999, aged 20, in a 46–10 defeat by Australia in Brisbane. In 2003 he was the natural successor to Keith Wood as the captain of his country, and in his first year as skipper led the Irish to Triple Crown success. O'Driscoll is so popular that many Irish fans wear T-shirts bearing the motto "In BOD We Trust". He has been capped six times by the British Lions and is one of the best centres ever to play the game.

## ℘ WIT AND WISDOM OF RUGBY (8) ℘

"Get your retaliation in first."
*Carwyn James*

## ℘ THE DUKES ℘

The British army's Duke of Wellington Regiment has a proud and illustrious Rugby Union tradition. The "Dukes" produced three players who were chosen for the British Lions, seven English internationals, three Scottish internationals and one Irish international. The "Dukes" produced some formidable sides in their history, winning the Army Cup no fewer than 14 times and finishing runners-up eight times.

## ℘ THE ENGLISH PITBULL ℘

Former England hooker Brian Moore, who won 64 caps for England between 1987 and 1995, was nicknamed "Pitbull" during his playing career. When asked once how he came to get the nickname, Moore explained: "My nickname came from Wade Dooley, the Blackpool policeman [and former England lock]. I don't know why he came up with it particularly. Some said it was a remarkable resemblance to the horrible beasts. Others said it was because of an attitude of never wanting to let go of something once you'd got hold of it. But it was probably a combination of both really."

*Did You Know That?*
England team-mate Paul Rendall described Moore's crooked front teeth as "the kind you get from a DIY shop and hammer in yourself".

## ℘ THREE CAPTAINS FOR THE CHAMPIONS ℘

Sam Warburton captained Wales in their opening-match loss to Ireland in the 2013 RBS Six Nations Championship. Unfortunately, he picked up an injury and missed the next game, against France in Paris. Ryan Jones took over as captain, and although Warburton returned for the match against Italy, Jones retained the captaincy and was told he would remain skipper for the rest of the tournament. However, Jones sustained a shoulder injury against Scotland and missed the deciding game against England at the Millennium Stadium, Cardiff. Although he was fit again and in the starting line-up, the captaincy did not return to Warburton, but went to prop forward Gethin Jenkins instead.

*O*

## "TRIPLE CROWN"

The origins of the name "Triple Crown" are obscure. However, the first recorded use of the term appeared in the *Irish Times* on 12 March 1894, following an Ireland victory over Wales: "After long years of seemingly hopeful struggle Ireland has achieved the Triple Crown honours of Rugby football. For the first time in the annals of the game have the Hibernians proved beyond cavil or doubt their right to be dubbed champions of the nations and that the Irishmen fully deserve the great distinction no one will deny ... Hurrah for Hibernia!"

## SPRING IS IN THE AIR

The RBS Six Nations Championship is contested each season over seven weekends during February, March and sometimes April.

## TALKING WALES

Since 2004 Jonathan Davies (32 caps for Wales 1985–97) has hosted his own rugby-themed chat show on the Welsh-language television channel S4C, shown on the evening before an international match involving Wales.

## WHEN PHIL MADE HISTORY

Phil Bennett made 29 appearances for Wales between 1969 and 1978, eight as captain. Although most of his games were at fly-half, he was sometimes used at full-back and centre. Phil made his debut on 22 March 1969 in Wales's 8–8 Five Nations Championship draw with France at the Stade Olympique Yves-du-Manoir, Colombes. Wales won the Five Nations Championship and Triple Crown in 1969. When Bennett came on as a substitute he became the first ever substitute in the history of international Rugby Union. Phil possessed a famous side-step and vicious body swerve that left many of his opponents clutching nothing but air as he glided past them. In 1974 Phil toured South Africa with the British Lions (won 3–0) and scored 103 points. Three years later he captained the Lions tour of Fiji (lost 1–0) and New Zealand (lost 3–1). During his career Phil also played for the Barbarians 20 times, including their famous 1973 win against New Zealand when he was involved in the move leading to Gareth Edwards's legendary try. Bennett played for Llanelli RFC for 16 years and in 2005 was inducted into the Welsh Rugby Hall of Fame. He won three Grand Slams and four Triple Crowns with Wales.

## ❧ ENGLAND AT HOME ❧

England has played a home international Rugby Union match at the following grounds: Whalley Range ❖ Blackheath ❖ Richmond ❖ Headingley ❖ Fallowfield ❖ Twickenham.

## ❧ WELSH DRAGON ALL PUFFED OUT ❧

Wales went into the 2013 Six Nations Championship as the reigning champions and looking to complete back-to-back Grand Slams. Those Grand Slam dreams ended with a 30–22 opening-game defeat against Ireland in Cardiff. Worse than that, having lost all four of their autumn internationals, it was Wales's first ever five-game losing streak.

## ❧ AN ITALIAN HOME ❧

Stadio Flaminio was home to Italian rugby up to 2011. It was built in 1959 and hosted the final of the 1960 Olympic Games Football tournament. Flaminio hosted all of Italy's Six Nations games from 2000 to 2011 when the Italian Rugby Federation decided to move to the much bigger Stadio Olimpico across the city.

*Did You Know That?*
Italy faced Australia in Genoa in 2000 and New Zealand in Florence in 2010 and both autumn internationals attracted 40,000 crowds.

## ❧ A SPORTING FAMILY ❧

Jean-Claude Skrela, the son of Polish refugees, played 46 times for France as a back-row forward, winning the Five Nations Championship and the Grand Slam in 1977. In 1995 he succeeded Pierre Berbizier as the coach of the French national team and coached the French to their first back-to-back Grand Slam titles in 1997 and 1998. However, when France was awarded the wooden spoon in 1999 he resigned and was replaced by Bernard Laporte later that year. His son, David, won his first cap for France in 2001, while his daughter, Gaëlle Skrela, is a professional basketball player.

## ❧ ALTERNATE HOME ADVANTAGE ❧

In the Six Nations Championship each nation plays the other five once per season, with home advantage alternating (e.g. Ireland hosted England in 2013, so the Irish will travel to Twickenham in 2014).

## ♆ A DRAMATIC FINAL DAY ♆

Going into the final round of matches in the 2007 RBS Six Nations Championship, all three games were played on the same day, with four teams, England, France, Ireland and Italy, all in with a chance of winning the tournament. The French led the table on points difference from Ireland, while both England and Italy had a chance of being crowned champions if they won by a large margin and the other results favoured them. Up first was Ireland versus Italy at the Stadio Flaminio in Rome, with the Irish coming away with an impressive 54–21 victory. The second game was between France and Scotland at the Stade de France, Paris, with Elvis Vermeulen scoring a try in the final minute to give the French a 45–19 victory and the 2007 Six Nations Championship by a slender +4 points advantage over Ireland. In the final game of a quite nail-biting day, England needed to beat Wales by 57 points in Cardiff to overtake France. However, the Welsh were more concerned about avoiding the indignity of being awarded the wooden spoon, and they beat their visitors 27–18 to hand the title to the French and the spoon to Scotland.

*Did You Know That?*
As time was running out in Rome Ireland were in possession of the ball and could have kicked into touch to end the game and thereby leave the French needing to beat Scotland by 30 points in their game. However, the Irish elected to go for another try, only for Italy to regain possession and score a converted try, reducing France's winning margin target to 23 points.

## ♆ WORDS OF WISDOM ♆

Gareth Edwards recalls the words of the great Welsh international, Cliff Morgan, when, following a trial match for Wales in 1966, Gareth was not selected for the Welsh side in their next international: "I played in the trial and I remember Cliff Morgan wrote a piece which I never forgot. He said, 'Gareth Edwards might not win his cap in the next match, but I believe he will win dozens in years to come', and that was great. It took away the disappointment of not being in the team."

*Did You Know That?*
Edwards was one of four Welshmen among 15 inductees into the inaugural class of the International Rugby Hall of Fame in 1997. His three compatriots were Morgan, J. P. R. Williams and Barry John.

## 🎵 WALES RUGBY ANTHEM 🎵

"Land of My Fathers" is the traditional national anthem of Wales. It was written in 1856 by Evan James, whose son James composed the music. The James family was from Pontypridd, Glamorgan.

**Hen Wlad Fy Nhadau (Land of My Fathers)**
Mae hen wlad fy nhadau yn annwyl i mi,
Gwlad beirdd a chantorion, enwogion o fri;
Ei gwrol ryfelwyr, gwladgarwyr tra mâd,
Dros ryddid collasant eu gwaed.

(Cytgan – chorus)

Gwlad, gwlad, pleidiol wyf I'm gwlad.

Tra môr yn fur I'r bur hoff bau,

O bydded I'r hen iaith barhau.

Hen Gymru fynyddig, paradwys y bardd,
Pob dyffryn, pob clogwyn, i'm golwg sydd hardd;
Trwy deimlad gwladgarol, mor swynol yw si
Ei nentydd, afonydd, i mi.

(Cytgan)

Os treisiodd y gelyn fy ngwlad tan ei droed,
Mae hen iaith y Cymry mor fyw ag erioed,
Ni luddiwyd yr awen gan erchyll law brad,
Na thelyn berseiniol fy ngwlad.

(Cytgan)

## 🎵 THE MERCHANT OF KELSO 🎵

Gavin Roger Todd Baird, born in Kelso on 12 April 1960, won 27 caps for Scotland on the wing between 1981 and 1988. He was first capped by his country in their 24–15 win over Australia at Murrayfield in 1981 and also represented the British Lions in 1983 (a series lost 4–0 to the All Blacks), playing in all four Tests and scoring six tries in 11 appearances. Baird, a grain merchant by trade, also managed the Scotland Under-21 side.

## ❧ THE MAGNIFICENT 15 ❧

The RBS Six Nations Championship comprises a total of 15 matches per tournament.

## ❧ BLOODY SUNDAY ❧

On 24 February 2007, Ireland welcomed England to Croke Park, the home of the Gaelic Athletic Association, for Ireland's home Six Nations Championship game. (Lansdowne Road, the home of Irish rugby, was undergoing redevelopment work at the time.) It was only the second ever Rugby Union game played at the famous Dublin stadium, and in the lead-up to the game a number of Irish politicians expressed their concerns over the proposed fixture, given the events of "Bloody Sunday 1920". The politicians were concerned about possible crowd reaction to the singing of "God Save the Queen". In the end the anthem was sung uninterrupted, after which the Irish went on to hammer England 43–13 to record their best ever victory over their rivals.

*Did You Know That?*
"Bloody Sunday 1920" is the name given to the events that occurred on 21 November 1920 during the Irish War of Independence (1919–21) which left 31 people dead. Firstly the Irish Republican Army killed 14 people who were members, or informants, of a British intelligence network known as the Cairo Gang. This was followed by the British army opening fire on a crowd attending a Gaelic football match at Croke Park, resulting in the deaths of 14 civilians. Later the same evening, three Irishmen held prisoner in Dublin Castle met their deaths under very suspicious circumstances.

## ❧ WHEN 20 BECAME 15 ❧

When the first ever Rugby Union international was contested between England and Scotland in 1871, the game was played 20-a-side. In 1876, the number of players per team was reduced to 15 after Oxford University persuaded their rivals Cambridge University to play the Varsity Match with just 15 players per side in 1875. Oxford's suggestion was an immediate success, as it opened up space in which to run with the ball, and after two consecutive draws in the fixture the game was won by Oxford. The first international with 15 players on each team was the England versus Ireland game in 1877.

## ✍ AN HONORARY WELSHMAN ✍

David Duckham is one of England's greatest players of all time. He made his debut on 8 February 1969 in a 17–15 defeat to Ireland at Lansdowne Road, Dublin, in the Five Nations Championship. Duckham played at centre alongside John Spencer and was a player who possessed not only a wonderfully teasing side-step and an aggressive hand-off but also pace and vision. Unfortunately for Duckham, he played in an era when the England team was incessantly chopped and changed in an attempt to compete with the Welsh, who ruled European rugby at the time. "There was not one of us who felt that his place was secure. The side was never settled and morale was pitifully low," said Duckham, when asked about his England career from 1969 to 1976. Duckham was capped 36 times by England but was on the winning side on only 10 of those occasions, scoring 10 tries. However, he excelled in the famous red jersey of the British Lions and especially on the 1971 tour of New Zealand, when he once scored six tries for the mid-week side, a record for a single game that he holds to this day (jointly, since 1974, with Wales's J. J. Williams). He scored 11 tries in his 16 games on the victorious 1971 tour, winning three Lions caps. He was the only English back in the 1973 Barbarians team that famously beat the mighty All Blacks 23–11 at the Arms Park, after which he was rechristened "Dai" by the Welsh fans because he played like "one of our own". On 21 February 1976, he made his last appearance for England, a 22–12 defeat to Scotland in the Five Nations Championship (England were awarded the wooden spoon). Duckham played for Coventry RFC for 12 seasons from 1967 to 1979, and in 1977 he was awarded the MBE for his services to rugby. Duckham is today an honorary president of the rugby charity Wooden Spoon, which helps improve the lives of disadvantaged children and young people in Britain and Ireland.

***Did You Know That?***
Duckham was also nicknamed "the Blond Bombshell".

## ✍ THE FIR ✍

On 25 July 1911, a "Propaganda Committee" was created to promote Rugby Union in Italy. In 1928 this became the Italian Rugby Federation, or *Federazione Italiana Rugby* (FIR), the governing body for Rugby Union in Italy. In 1987 the FIR joined the International Rugby Board when Italy participated in the inaugural Rugby World Cup.

## ✺ PELOUS HONOURED BY IRB ✺

On 21 October 2007, France's Fabien Pelous was awarded the IRPA Special Merit Award for his services to rugby at the annual IRB Awards ceremony held in Paris. In a year dominated by the southern hemisphere teams, South Africa winning the Rugby World Cup, Pelous was the only Six Nations player or coach honoured at the event. Pelous was capped 118 times by France (42 as captain) and played his last international for his country in France's semi-final loss to England in the 2007 Rugby World Cup.

*Did You Know That?*
Pelous captained Stade Toulousain to Heineken Cup glory in 2005.

## ✺ CAPTAIN FANTASTIC ✺

In the autumn of 2003, Jason Robinson was appointed the 118th captain of England, thereby becoming the first mixed-race player and the first former Rugby League player to captain England. Robinson celebrated his captaincy with a hat-trick of tries in the 70–0 whitewash of Canada.

## ✺ A QUESTION OF SPORT ✺

*A Question of Sport* first appeared on our television screens on 5 January 1970. On the first show, which was hosted by David Vine, the team captains Henry Cooper and Cliff Morgan were joined by George Best, Ray Illingworth, Lillian Board and Tom Finney. More than 1,000 sporting personalities have appeared on the programme in its 43-year history, led by 14 resident captains. In addition to Cliff Morgan several other rugby legends have been team captains: Gareth Edwards (Wales), Bill Beaumont (England) and Matt Dawson (England).

## ✺ THE SCULPTOR ✺

Jean-Pierre Rives, the former French rugby captain, has been a sculptor for more than 30 years. During the early 1980s (Jean-Pierre did not retire from playing rugby until December 1984) he met the sculptor Albert Féraud, who instantly altered Rives's vision of life and the world. Today, Jean-Pierre's sculptures can be found among major collections across the globe, including Cap Gemini's at La Fontaine. Jean-Pierre is the first sculptor since Rodin to have a solo exhibition in the Jardins du Luxembourg in Paris.

## ❧ WIT AND WISDOM OF RUGBY (9) ❧

"We've lost seven of our last eight matches. Only team that we've beaten was Western Samoa. Good job we didn't play the whole of Samoa."
**Gareth Davies**

## ❧ SING YOUR HEARTS OUT ❧

Each one of the six nations competing in the RBS Six Nations Championship has its own anthem/national anthem:
England: "God Save the Queen"
France: "La Marseillaise (The Song of Marseilles)"
Ireland: "A Soldier's Song"
Italy: "Il Canto degli Italiani (The Song of the Italians)"
Scotland: "Flower of Scotland (Flùr na h-Alba)"
Wales: "Hen Wlad Fy Nhadau (Land of My Fathers)"

## ❧ THE JEWELS OF THE EMERALD ISLE ❧

Ronan O'Gara, Peter Stringer, John Hayes, Simon Easterby and Shane Horgan all made their international debuts for Ireland against Scotland on 19 February 2000 in the inaugural Six Nations Championship. Ireland's 44–22 win that day at Lansdowne Road, Dublin, established a new Irish record for a defeat of the Scots at the time (Ireland won 36–6 in Dublin in 2003), eclipsing their 21–0 victory in Dublin on 25 February 1950 in the Five Nations Championship.

*Did You Know That?*
Up to the end of the 2013 Six Nations Championship, the Ireland v Scotland fixture is the third most played match in the history of international rugby. In 2013, they had met for the 128th time. Top of the list is Australia v New Zealand with 146 games, while England v Scotland comes second with 131 games.

## ❧ A MEMORABLE HALF-CENTURY ❧

On 24 February 2007, Andrea Lo Cicero made his 50th appearance for the *Azzurri* when they faced Scotland at Murrayfield in the Six Nations Championship. The game, in which the Italians triumphed 37–12, entered into Italian rugby history books because, at the 20th attempt, this was their first ever away victory since entering the Six Nations in 2000.

# ❧ CUPS WITHIN A CUP ❧

Within each Six Nations Championship six other competitions take place. Since 1879 England and Scotland have competed for the Calcutta Cup, and since 1988 the Millennium Trophy has been awarded to the winner of the game between England and Ireland. In 2007 France and Italy introduced their own prize, the Giuseppe Garibaldi Trophy. Meanwhile, the Centenary Quaich is contested annually by Ireland and Scotland. The original "Home Nations" compete for the Triple Crown, while any nation that wins all five of their games wins the coveted Grand Slam title.

***Did You Know That?***
The Giuseppe Garibaldi Trophy was introduced to commemorate the 200th anniversary of Giuseppe Garibaldi, the Italian revolutionary hero who helped unify Italy and who was born in Nizza, Italy, in 1807. Nizza subsequently came under French rule, with the current name of Nice adopted in 1859.

# ❧ JASON'S DOUBLE GONG ❧

Former England international Jason Robinson was appointed an Officer of the British Empire (OBE) in the 2008 New Year Honours list, having previously been awarded an MBE in 2003 following England's Rugby World Cup win.

# ❧ SIR CLIVE BY THE NUMBERS ❧

During Sir Clive Woodward's seven years as coach of the national team, England scored 2,886 points, conceded 1,490 points, scored 320 tries and allowed their opponents to score 142. His win percentage was 71.1 per cent (P83, W59, D2, L22).

# ❧ NO. 13 SHIRT RETIRED ❧

Ivan Francescato made his debut for Italy on 7 October 1990 against Romania, thereby becoming the fourth of six brothers to play at senior international level for the *Azzurri*, following Bruno, Nello and Rino. He played his final game for his country on 8 November 1997 against South Africa, having won 38 caps and scored 77 points. On 19 January 1999, at the age of 31, Ivan died of a heart attack, whereupon the Treviso rugby board decided to retire his No. 13 shirt for the season (he played his entire career for Benetton Treviso).

## ❧ EPIC GAMES (6) ☙

### 1971 – SCOTLAND 18, WALES 19

Going into the final minutes of the game the Welsh trailed the Scots by four points at Murrayfield. However, Wales's flying wing, Gerald Davies, received a long pass and ran up the field to score. Then up stepped John Taylor who coolly sent the conversion sailing through the uprights from 10 yards inside touch to secure victory for the visitors. Wales went on to win the first of three Grand Slams during the decade, and so began a new golden age of Welsh rugby, based on the magnificent half-back pairing of Gareth Edwards and Barry John. The *Daily Telegraph* described the epic at Murrayfield as "one of the great games of a lifetime".

***Did You Know That?***
In Wales's 1971 Grand Slam-winning season the other four nations managed only one victory each (Scotland took the wooden spoon).

## ❧ IF YOU KNOW YOUR HISTORY – 6 ☙

In 1910 France, who had played in four of the original Home International Championships up to that point, officially joined the competition – and the "Five Nations" came into being.

## ❧ THE SCOTTISH LION ☙

Ian McGeechan, a future Scotland and British Lions coach, made his debut for Scotland in the 1972 Five Nations Championship and went on to win 32 caps (and score 21 points) for his country at fly-half and centre, captaining the side nine times. He also won eight caps for the British Lions on their 1974 and 1977 tours.

## ❧ THE DRAGON'S STATISTICS ☙

When Gareth Thomas became the first Welsh player to win 100 caps after captaining his country in a 38–34 loss to Fiji at the Stade de La Baujoire Stadium, Nantes, for their Pool B game during the 2007 Rugby World Cup, he had amassed a record of 51 wins, 1 draw and 48 defeats. In the 100 games Thomas led Wales out as captain 21 times, winning 9 of those matches, losing 11 and drawing 1. He played 19 matches at full-back, 55 on the wing and 20 at centre, while the remaining 6 appearances (all as a replacement) saw him play twice more in each of those three positions.

# ৡৢ MARTIN JOHNSON – AN ENGLISH LION ৡৢ

Martin Osborne Johnson was born on 9 March 1970 in Solihull, West Midlands. In 1987 he was selected by England Schools and, the following year, joined Leicester Youth as a lock forward. England Colts honours and his Leicester first-team debut came his way in 1989–90. In the summer of 1990 former All Black Colin Meads, the head coach of the King Country club in New Zealand, invited Johnson for a trial, and after impressing there he was signed up. He played two seasons for the side in the Inter Provincial Championship Second Division and, in 1991, was selected to play for the New Zealand Under-21 side which toured Australia. Johnson returned to England in September 1991 and won England Under-21 honours, playing in a 94–0 win over Belgium.

Johnson played in "B" international matches against France and Italy before receiving a senior England call-up on 16 January 1993, when an injury forced Wade Dooley to withdraw from the team to face France at Twickenham. England beat the French 16–15, with Johnson acquitting himself well. Four months later, he helped Leicester to Pilkington Cup glory, scoring a try in the final against Harlequins. In June 1993, another injury to Wade Dooley resulted in an unexpected call-up for Johnson to join the British Lions on tour in New Zealand and he played in the final two Tests. Johnson helped England to Triple Crown and Grand Slam glory in 1995. At the 1995 Rugby World Cup in South Africa he was the only England forward to play throughout their six matches in the tournament. Johnson was appointed captain of Leicester when Dean Richards retired, and Ian McGeechan made him the captain of the Lions for the 1997 tour of South Africa – although he was not England skipper, and they returned home 2–1 series winners.

Johnson became captain of England in June 1999 and, three months later, led England to the quarter-finals of the World Cup. Injury caused him to miss the 2000 Six Nations, but he returned to captain England for their 2001 Six Nations campaign and then went on to lead the British & Irish Lions on their 2001 tour to Australia.

In 2003 he had the year of all years: captaining England to a Six Nations Grand Slam, a 15–13 win over the All Blacks, the first in New Zealand for 30 years, a first ever win (25–14) over the Wallabies in Australia, and the ultimate prize of the Rugby World Cup. He retired from international rugby in January 2004 (84 caps, 10 points). On 16 April 2008 Johnson was appointed head coach of England, but he resigned after England's poor showing in the 2011 Rugby World Cup.

### Did You Know That?
Johnson was the first player to be named captain for two Lions tours.

## ❧ CARDS INTRODUCED ❧

The issuing of yellow and red cards in Rugby Union was introduced by the IRB in the 2000–01 season. When a player is shown a yellow card he is suspended from the game (sent to the sin bin) for 10 minutes. The suspension lasts for 10 minutes of actual playing time, so if the clock stops for any reason during the next 10 minutes then the 10-minute suspension period is also placed on hold. When a player is shown a red card he is sent off and must immediately leave the field of play.

## ❧ A QUESTION OF PRIORITIES ❧

In 2004 Matt Dawson, then England's regular scrum-half, followed in the footsteps of former England skipper Bill Beaumont as a resident captain on the popular BBC show *A Question of Sport*. However, Dawson's recording commitments soon got him into trouble, for in October that year he had to inform coach Andy Robinson that filming obligations would confine him to the TV studio on the day of an England training session. A totally unimpressed Robinson dropped Dawson from the team.

## ❧ THERE AND BACK AGAIN ❧

In 2001 Iestyn Harris, born in Oldham, Lancashire, made a £1.5m switch from Rugby League to Rugby Union when he left Leeds Rhinos and joined Cardiff Blues. On 10 November 2001, he made his debut for Wales in a 30–16 defeat by Argentina at the Millennium Stadium, Cardiff. Amazingly, he had played fewer than 200 hours of Rugby Union before his Welsh debut. He made 25 appearances for Wales, scoring 108 points between 2001 and 2004, when he went back to Rugby League, signing for the Bradford Bulls.

*Did You Know That?*
In 2005 Iestyn Harris wrote a book entitled *There and Back – My Journey from League to Union and Back Again*.

## ❧ KEEP YOUR CAP ON ❧

On 7 February 1885, Scotland were leading Ireland by one try to nil in Belfast in their Home Nations Championship game when the match was abandoned. The match was replayed two weeks later, with Scotland winning 1–0. Caps were awarded for both of the matches.

## ❧ FANTASY TEAMS – IRELAND XV ❧

**1**
Ray
*McLOUGHLIN*

**2**
Keith
*WOOD*

**3**
Phil
*ORR*

**4**
Willie John *McBRIDE*
*(capt)*

**5**
Donal
*LENIHAN*

**6**
Fergus
*SLATTERY*

**7**
John
*O'DRISCOLL*

**8**
Willie
*DUGGAN*

**9**
Peter
*STRINGER*

**10**
Jack
*KYLE*

**11**
Simon
*GEOGHEGAN*

**12**
Mike
*GIBSON*

**13**
Brian
*O'DRISCOLL*

**14**
Tony
*O'REILLY*

**15**
Tom
*KIERNAN*

*Replacements*

*16 Rob HENDERSON* ❖ *17 Ronan O'GARA* ❖ *18 Moss KEANE*
*19 Jeremy DAVIDSON* ❖ *20 Paul WALLACE* ❖ *21 Shane BYRNE*
*22 Nick POPPLEWELL* ❖ *23 Paul O'CONNELL*

*Coach*
*Eddie O'SULLIVAN*

*Did You Know That?*
Eddie O'Sullivan's first international coaching job at senior level was
with the US Eagles.

## ❧ ENGLAND 7, WALES 7 ❧

In 1976 Wales won the Five Nations Championship Grand Slam for
the seventh time to draw level with England at the top of the list of
Grand Slam winners.

## ❧ AN OFFICER AND A GENTLEMAN ❧

A Rugby World Cup winner with England in 2003, Josh Lewsey
had graduated from the Royal Military Academy at Sandhurst in
2001 and served for two years as an officer in the Royal Artillery
Regiment before deciding to pursue a career in Rugby Union.

## ❧ TRIPLE CROWN HISTORY ❧

The four Home Unions have been competing against each other for 125 years, since the first international between England and Wales in 1882. Wales were the first ever winners of the Triple Crown in 1893.

## ❧ KIDNEY FAILURE ❧

Declan Kidney was sacked as Ireland's coach after the team had finished fifth in the 2013 Six Nations Championship, avoiding the wooden spoon only because their points difference was nine better than France's. Kidney succeeded a fellow County Cork coach, Eddie O'Sullivan, in 2008 and, in his first season, he took Ireland to their first Grand Slam in 61 years. Despite the poor showing in 2013, the Irish had been the only team to defeat eventual champions Wales. Ireland won 14 of the 25 Six Nations Championship matches in the Kidney era and had two draws and nine defeats, a 60 per cent success rate. Under Kidney, Ireland's overall record was 27 wins and three draws in 53 matches, 1,128 points scored and 964 conceded.

## ❧ THE WELSH CENTURION ❧

On 29 September 2007, Gareth Thomas became the first Welsh player to win 100 caps when he led the team out against Fiji at the Stade de La Baujoire Stadium, Nantes, for their Pool B game during the 2007 Rugby World Cup. Sadly for the Welsh captain, Fiji won the game 38–34, a result that sent Wales crashing out of the competition. It was also Thomas's last game for his country. However, on a brighter note, Thomas managed to raise his international try-scoring total to 40 tries for Wales during the second half of the game. Thomas became only the eighth player to win a century of caps for his country, joining George Gregan (Australia), Fabien Pelous (France), Jason Leonard (England), Philippe Sella (France), Stephen Larkham (Australia), David Campese (Australia) and Alessandro Troncon (Italy). Thomas made 94 starts and was a replacement six times.

## ❧ FAMILY TIES ❧

When Phil Davies made his debut for Wales on 20 April 1985 in a 24–15 win over England at the National Stadium, Cardiff, in the Five Nations Championship, his brother-in-law, Jonathan Davies, was also winning his first cap.

## ❧ GRAND SLAMS (5) – FRANCE 1968 ❧

No match in France's first Grand Slam season was won by more than ten points. They beat Scotland 8–6 at Murrayfield before enjoying the biggest win of that season's Five Nations Championship, 16–6 over Ireland in Paris. After beating England 14–9 in Paris, France claimed *Le Grand Chelem* in a mudbath at Cardiff Arms Park. Lilian Camberabero and Christian Carrere scored tries, while Guy Camberabero added a penalty, drop goal and conversion as France turned a 9–3 deficit into a 14–11 victory.

### FIVE NATIONS CHAMPIONSHIP 1968

| Team | P | W | D | L | PF | PA | Pts |
|------|---|---|---|---|-----|-----|-----|
| France | 4 | 4 | 0 | 0 | 77 | 37 | 8 |
| Ireland | 4 | 2 | 1 | 1 | 38 | 37 | 5 |
| England | 4 | 1 | 2 | 1 | 37 | 40 | 4 |
| Wales | 4 | 1 | 1 | 2 | 31 | 34 | 3 |
| Scotland | 4 | 0 | 0 | 4 | 18 | 35 | 0 |

### RESULTS 1968 – COACH: JEAN PRAT

| Date | Venue | Opponent | Score | Captains |
|------|-------|----------|-------|----------|
| 24 January | Edinburgh | Scotland | 25–4 | C Carrere |
| 7 February | Swansea | Wales | 24–14 | C Carrere |
| 28 February | Dublin | Ireland | 14–8 | C Carrere |
| 15 March | Edinburgh | England | 14–11 | C Carrere |

*Did You Know That?*
France used 27 players in the four matches with only Christian Carrere, Walter Spanghero, Elie Cester and Andre Campaes appearing in every game.

## ❧ SCOTLAND'S GREAT WHITE SHARK ❧

John Jeffrey, nicknamed "the White Shark" because of his distinctive blond hair, won 40 caps for Scotland as a flanker (at the time Scotland's most capped flanker) between 1984 and 1991. Jeffrey was as brave as they come, a ferocious tackler and possessed such stamina that he was still making penetrating runs deep into the game when most others around him were sucking in air. He scored 11 tries and was a key member of their 1990 Grand Slam-winning side. Jeffrey made his Scotland debut on 8 December 1984 in a 34–12 defeat by Australia at Murrayfield and made his final appearance in their third-place play-off 13–6 loss to New Zealand in Cardiff at the 1991 Rugby World Cup.

# ℘ CELEBRITY RUGBY PLAYERS ℘

Over the years many notable celebrities from various walks of life have at some time or another enjoyed or endured the sport of rugby. Here are just a few of them:

**Idi Amin** – the former brutal dictator who ruled Uganda from 1971 to 1979 played for the Ugandan Test team as a hooker in 1956 and for the first team at Sandhurst Military College in England.

**Sir Douglas Bader** – the famous RAF fighter pilot who lost his legs in a flying accident represented the RAF College and played for Harlequins.

**Rt Hon. Gordon Brown, MP** – an article in the *Washington Post* refers to the British Prime Minister's association with the sport: "Brown was a bookish whiz kid from a mining and linoleum-producing town in Scotland. He entered the University of Edinburgh at 16, one of the school's youngest-ever students. A rugby injury when he was a teenager left him blind in his left eye; when he gives speeches, he uses notes printed in extra-large type. Friends said the injury only increased his determination to succeed."

**Richard Burton** – the legendary actor played rugby while growing up in South Wales.

**George W. Bush** – the former US president played rugby at Yale University.

**Raymond Chandler** – the American crime novelist played rugby while a schoolboy at Dulwich College in London in 1900–05.

**Charlie Chaplin** – the famous comic actor played rugby during his schooldays in England.

**Jacques Chirac** – the president of France from 1995 to 2007 played for the youth team of French First Division club Brive and later at university level.

**Sir Winston Churchill** – Britain's wartime leader is said to have hated playing rugby during his time at Sandhurst Military College.

**Bill Clinton** – the former US president played rugby in England from 1968 to 1970, when a part-time student at Oxford University.

**Sir Sean Connery** – played rugby at school in Scotland.

**Sir Arthur Conan Doyle** – the creator of the world's most famous fictional detective. One of the Sherlock Holmes stories is entitled *The Adventure of the Missing Three-Quarter*, while Holmes's sidekick, Dr John Watson, is said to have played rugby for Blackheath.

**Brian Epstein** – the legendary manager of the Beatles.

**Stephen Fry** – the actor played rugby in school but detested it. In his autobiography he described sport as "tribal shit".

**Ernesto "Che" Guevara** – the famous Marxist Argentinian-born guerrilla played rugby as a lad.

**Richard Harris** – the Irish actor who portrayed a rugby league player in the film *This Sporting Life* had played rugby union himself in his youth.

**Sir Edmund Hillary** – the conqueror of Mount Everest played full-back for Auckland Grammar School in New Zealand during the 1930s.

**Boris Karloff** – the famous star of classic Hollywood horror films.

**John F. Kennedy** – the Irish-American US president played rugby at Harvard University.

**Yoshio Mori** – the former Japanese prime minister.

**Matthew Pinsent** – the British rower, who won four Olympic gold medals in the coxless pairs, played second row for his school Eton and played club rugby for Henley before concentrating on rowing.

**Gary Player** – the legendary South African golfer.

**Daniel Radcliffe** – the actor who plays the hero in the Harry Potter films.

**Trevor Rees-Jones** – the former bodyguard of Diana, Princess of Wales.

**Jacques Rogge** – the president of the International Olympic Committee.

**Mike Tindall** – the England Rugby World Cup-winning centre married Olympic Equestrian silver medallist Zara Phillips, the Queen's grand-daughter, and 14th in line to the British throne.

**J. R. R. Tolkien** – the South African-born author of *The Lord of the Rings* played rugby in his schooldays.

**Sir P. G. Wodehouse** – the creator of Jeeves and Wooster among others played at scrum-half for Dulwich College, in London, in the late nineteenth century.

## ❧ IF YOU KNOW YOUR HISTORY – 7 ❧

England won the first Five Nations Championship of the new era, with France as official participators, in 1910.

## ❧ WOODEN SPOON JOY FOR ITALY ❧

Although Italy took a seventh consecutive Six Nations Championship wooden spoon in 2006, after joining the expanded tournament in 2000, they did manage to collect their first point away from home when they drew with Wales at the Millennium Stadium.

## ❧ "SWING LOW, SWEET CHARIOT" ☙

On 5 March 1988, England's first black player for 80 years, Chris Oti, made his debut in a 9–6 defeat of Scotland at Murrayfield in the Five Nations Championship. Two weeks later Oti made his indelible mark on English rugby when he scored a super hat-trick against Ireland in England's 35–3 Five Nations Championship win at Twickenham. When Oti touched down for his final try of the game a group from the Benedictine school Douai began singing the 150-year-old hymn "Swing Low, Sweet Chariot", a song they always sang for their own rugby team. The entire crowd joined in, and it has remained the England fans' unofficial anthem ever since:

*Chorus*
Swing low, sweet chariot
Coming for to carry me home
Swing low, sweet chariot
Coming for to carry me home

I looked over Jordan and what did I see
Coming for to carry me home
A band of angels coming after me
Coming for to carry me home
*Chorus*
Sometimes I'm up and sometimes I'm down
Coming for to carry me home
But still my soul feels heavenly bound
Coming for to carry me home
*Chorus*
The brightest day that I can say
Coming for to carry me home
When Jesus washed my sins away
Coming for to carry me home
*Chorus*
If I get there before you do
Coming for to carry me home
I'll cut a hole and pull you through
Coming for to carry me home
*Chorus*
If you get there before I do
Coming for to carry me home
Tell all my friends I'm coming too
Coming for to carry me home
*Chorus*

## ✌ WHO DARES WINS ✌

If two or more teams finish an RBS Six Nations Championship with the same number of points, the winning nation is decided on match-points difference (subtracting points "against" from points "for" in each nation's five championship matches). If this system does not produce a winner, then the trophy is awarded to the team who scored the most tries during the championship. However, if there is still no clear winner, then the trophy is shared.

## ✌ THE POINTS SYSTEM ✌

In the RBS Six Nations Championship two points are awarded for a win and one point for a draw.

## ✌ LUCKY 13 FOR WILL ✌

During his career England's Will Greenwood played at both inside centre and outside centre, but because of superstition he always wore the No. 13 jersey. In 1997 Will was not chosen to win his first cap by the England coach Jack Rowell for the Five Nations Championship but was selected for the British Lions tour to South Africa (won 2–1). During one game Will swallowed his tongue after a collision and stopped breathing for several minutes, and he did not appear in any of the Tests. In the game Will wore the No. 12 jersey.

## ✌ DEBUT HAT-TRICK ✌

Gareth Thomas made his debut for Wales against Japan in Bloemfontein in the 1995 Rugby World Cup, scoring a hat-trick of tries, and if he had not damaged his rib cartilage against Australia during Wales's tour of the country in the summer of 2007, then he would have won his 100th cap against the same opposition, Japan, on 20 September 2007 in Wales's 72–18 victory in their 2007 Rugby World Cup Pool B game at the Millennium Stadium, Cardiff.

## ✌ THE TOONIE FLIP ✌

The Toonie Flip is the name of the magnificent reverse pass which Gregor Townsend gave to team-mate Gavin Hastings, taking two French defenders out of the play in the process, enabling Scotland to claim a dramatic last-minute 23–21 win against France in Paris on 18 February 1995.

## ❧ RONAN'S YEAR ❧

Ireland's Ronan O'Gara topped the table in both tries scored and points scored during the 2007 RBS Six Nations Championship.

## ❧ FIRST FIVE NATIONS WOODEN SPOON ❧

France became the first team to win the wooden spoon in a Five Nations Championship when they finished bottom of the table in 1910. The French failed to win or even draw any of their four games, in which they scored 20 points and conceded 95 for a final total of -75.

## ❧ LOVE YOU JONNY ❧

In the 2006 Christmas-themed novel entitled *It's Cold Outside*, an entire chapter of the book is dedicated to the 2003 Rugby World Cup final in Sydney, punctuated with the infamous line "Love you Jonny" in homage to his winning drop goal against Australia.

## ❧ WALES'S FIRST TO WIN 50 MATCHES ❧

Gareth Thomas claimed his 50th win in a Welsh jersey, becoming the first Welsh player to reach that landmark, when he led his side to a 27–20 win over Argentina at the Millennium Stadium on 18 August 2007.

## ❧ COACH TURNED STATESMAN ❧

In 1999 Bernard Laporte was appointed the first fully professional head coach of France. During his playing career Laporte, a scrum-half, never won a full cap for France, but he did win the French Under-21 Championship with UA Gaillac in 1983 and was captain of the side that retained the title in 1984. In 1990, he captained Bègles-Bordeaux to the French Championship. When he took over the French national side he made Fabien Pelous the team captain, and on 5 February 2000 he won his first game as national coach, a 36–3 win over Wales at the Millennium Stadium, Cardiff, in the inaugural Six Nations Championship. In 2002 and 2004 he guided France to the Grand Slam, and in both 2006 and 2007 France were once again crowned Six Nations Champions. Following the 2007 Rugby World Cup Laporte resigned as national team coach to take up his new appointment as France's Secretary of State for Sport.

## ⚜ ENGLAND SLAMMED ⚜

The 1978 Five Nations Championship was the 49th series of the tournament, the 84th including the original Home Nations Championship series. The championship was won by Wales, who had now claimed the title 20 times (29 times including 9 shared titles), and having won all four of their games the Welsh also claimed their third consecutive Triple Crown, thereby becoming the first team to achieve this feat. More important for the Welsh was that it was a record 15th Triple Crown, one better than England's 14 Triple Crowns, and the sweetest statistic of all was that the Welsh had now won a record eight Grand Slams, also one more than England.

## ⚜ THE WELSH WHIPPET ⚜

In 1973 John James Williams won the first of his 30 caps for Wales (scoring 12 tries). However, J. J.'s first love in sport was athletics, and in 1970 he represented Wales at the Commonwealth Games in Edinburgh. He ran in the 100m heats (10.67 secs for fifth place behind Hasely Crawford from Trinidad, who won the Olympic gold medal in Montreal in 1976) and the 200m quarter-finals (finishing seventh in a race won by Don Quarrie, who won the gold medal over the same distance at the 1976 Olympic Games in Montreal) and was a member of the Welsh team that finished fifth in the final of the 4 x 100m relay (taking the baton from Lynn Davies on the third leg). John called himself "J. J." to distinguish himself from the other great John Williams in the all-conquering Welsh side of the 1970s, J. P. R. Williams, their swashbuckling full-back. He still shares two try-scoring records for the British Lions. At Monsel Bay in South Africa in 1974, he scored six tries against South-West Districts to equal the tally of England's David Duckham for the most tries by a Lion in a single match. He also scored four tries in four matches against the Springboks in 1974, to equal fellow countryman Willie Llewellyn's record for the most tries in a Test series – he scored 12 tries in 11 appearances during the Lions' 22-game tour (21 wins and 1 draw). His outstanding performances on the 1974 Lions tour earned him the nickname "the Welsh Whippet". J. J. won four consecutive Triple Crowns and two Grand Slams with Wales.

### Did You Know That?
All of J. J.'s children have represented Wales in track and field athletics, and his son Rhys was Britain's top 400m hurdler, reaching the semi-final of the 2005 World Championships at Helsinki.

## ✿ WIT AND WISDOM OF RUGBY (10) ✿

"Bloody typical, isn't it? The car's a write-off. The tanker's a write-off. But JPR comes out of it all in one piece."
**Gareth Edwards**, *after J. P. R. Williams was involved in a road traffic accident*

## ✿ KNOW YOUR BALLS ✿

All Rugby Union balls must be between 28 cm and 30 cm in length (approximately 11–13 ins), and most full-size balls weigh between 383 and 440 g (approximately 13.5–15.5 oz).

## ✿ DISPUTED TOURNAMENTS ✿

Before the turn of the twentieth century the Home International Championships were marred by disputes, and on three occasions, 1885, 1887 and 1889, the tournament could not be completed.

## ✿ DAWS ✿

During his international career Matthew Dawson, nicknamed "Daws", won 77 caps for England (including 9 as captain, scoring 101 points) and toured with the British Lions three times (7 caps, 10 points) and was a member of England's 2003 Rugby World Cup-winning team. Matt is England's most capped scrum-half.

## ✿ SCOTLAND'S SCRAP YARD DOG ✿

Gary Armstrong captained Scotland to Five Nations Championship success in 1999, the last ever Five Nations Championship before it became Six Nations. In August 1999, in a game against Romania, he equalled fellow Scot Roy Laidlaw's record for his country of 47 caps at scrum-half. Two months later, Armstrong celebrated his half-century of appearances for Scotland when he captained his country to victory in the World Cup play-off match against Samoa. Armstrong retired from international rugby after Scotland's 30–18 loss to the All Blacks in the quarter-finals of the 1999 Rugby World Cup, having won 51 caps and scored 21 points. He also played for the British Lions on their tour of Australia in 1989 (won 2–1). In Jonny Wilkinson's book *How to Play Rugby My Way*, the England outside half gave Gary the nickname "Scrap Yard Dog", claiming that he had never played against a tougher opponent than the Scot.

## ❧ EPIC GAMES (7) ❧

### 1980 – SCOTLAND 18, ENGLAND 30

England visited Murrayfield on 15 March 1980 knowing that a win over Scotland would give them their first outright Five Nations Championship since 1963 (there was a five-way tie in 1973) and, with it, the Triple Crown and Grand Slam. England, captained by Bill Beaumont, brought a miserable period for English rugby to an end with an emphatic 30–18 victory. The England back-line that day included Dusty Hare, Mike Slemen and England's future World Cup-winning coach, Clive Woodward. England's John Carleton was the man of the match, scoring three tries.

*Did You Know That?*
Scotland's defeat condemned them to the wooden spoon.

## ❧ TRIPLE CROWN QUAD ❧

Only two nations have won the coveted Triple Crown in four consecutive years, Wales from 1976 to 1979 and England from 1995 to 1998. No other nation has ever won the Triple Crown more than two years in succession.

## ❧ REPLACEMENTS INTRODUCED ❧

It was not until the 1968–69 season that the IRB amended the Laws to allow the replacement of injured players (up to two players per team). The first official replacement in a Test match came when Ireland's Mike Gibson replaced Wales's Barry John in the British Lions team during the first Test against South Africa in 1968 (unofficial replacements happened frequently in Australia, New Zealand and South Africa prior to this).

*Did You Know That?*
Tactical substitutions were introduced in 1996 (three per team).

## ❧ IT RUNS IN THE BLOOD ❧

In late 2007, Marc Lièvremont succeeded Bernard Laporte as the national coach of France. During his playing career he was capped at back-row forward 25 times by France between 1995 and 1999. Lièvremont has six younger brothers and one younger sister, all of whom play or played rugby at different levels.

# JONNY WILKINSON – AN ENGLISH HERO

Jonathan Peter Wilkinson was born on 25 May 1979 in Frimley, Surrey. Encouraged by his father, he began playing rugby when he was just four years old. Jonny was a gifted young sportsman, and at Pierrepont School and Lord Wandsworth College he also played cricket and tennis. He was an opening bowler and batsman for the school and played cricket for Hampshire Schools until rugby began to take up most of his time. He was selected for the England Under-16 rugby team, and he made a name for himself on England Under-18 Schools' tour of Australia in 1997, accumulating 94 points in five games. Jonny left school after that summer, but deferred studying at Durham University for a year to try his hand (and feet) at full-time rugby with the Newcastle Falcons.

Jonny made his international debut for England on 6 June 1998 against Australia in the Cook Cup in Brisbane. On 3 February 2001, he scored 18 points against Wales at the Millennium Stadium to reach 407 international points, overtaking Rob Andrew as England's all-time leading points scorer. Two weeks later, Jonny's 35 points against Italy in England's 90–23 victory at Twickenham (a record for the tournament) saw the fly-half surpass the single-game record of 30 points scored by Ronan O'Gara for Ireland against Italy in 2000. However, if ever there was a year that belonged to one rugby player, then 2003 was the Year of Jonny. After he had been awarded an MBE in the New Year Honours list, his dramatic winning drop goal against Australia in the last minute of extra time in the 2003 Rugby World Cup Final won the famous Webb Ellis trophy for England and made Wilkinson a superstar overnight. Endorsement opportunities arrived by the dozen, while the nation personally thanked him by voting him the BBC Sports Personality of the Year and, to top things off, he was also named the IRB International Player of the Year for 2003.

Injuries blighted the remainder of Jonny's international career, and he played only a handful of matches between 2003 and 2009, but he did set a new Calcutta Cup points record, scoring 27 in England's 42–20 defeat of Scotland at Twickenham in 2007 and, in 2008, during England's 23–19 defeat of Italy in Rome, passed the 1,000 international points mark. Jonny left Newcastle in 2009 and joined French club Toulon. After 91 appearances for England and six for the British Lions, he retired from international rugby. His career total of 1,246 points (1,179 for England) is second-best all-time, behind only New Zealand's Dan Carter.

### Did You Know That?
Jonny's kicking coach and mentor, David Alred, became an adviser to former world golf No.1 Luke Donald.

## ❦ IF YOU KNOW YOUR HISTORY – 8 ❧

In 1931 France were excluded from participating in the Five Nations tournament in a row over professionalism, and it reverted to being the "Home Nations Championships" from 1932 through to 1939.

## ❦ A HALF-CENTURY OF FIVE NATIONS ❧

The 1979 Five Nations Championship was the 50th series of the tournament, the 85th including the original Home Nations Championship series. Wales claimed the crown for the second successive year, and with their only loss coming to France, 14–13 in the National Stadium, Cardiff, the Welsh lifted their record 16th Triple Crown, which put them two ahead of nearest challengers England.

## ❦ *CELEBRITY MASTERCHEF* ❧

In September 2006, the former England scrum-half Matt Dawson won the BBC One television series *Celebrity Masterchef*, beating athlete Roger Black and Hardeep Singh Kohli (a Sikh broadcaster, reporter and writer) in the final.

## ❦ JUGGLING BAT AND BALL ❧

Rob Andrew, the former England fly-half, was also a talented cricketer (a left-handed batsman and right-arm off-break bowler), winning a blue in the sport at Cambridge. In addition to appearing for the Yorkshire Second XI several times he scored one first-class century, 101 not out against Nottinghamshire in July 1984. During one of his games for Yorkshire he dismissed, for a duck, a 17-year-old future England cricket captain – Mike Atherton.

## ❦ THE MAN FROM SEVEN SISTERS ❧

Phil Davies, born in Seven Sisters, Wales, in 1963, won 46 caps for Wales in an international career from 1985 to 1995. A versatile player, who was at home at flanker, lock forward or No. 8, Phil made his debut on 20 April 1985 in a 24–15 win over England at the National Stadium, Cardiff, in the Five Nations Championship. The win extended Wales's unbeaten run against England in Cardiff to 22 years. Wales won 50 per cent of their games with Phil in the side (P46, W23, D1, L22), and he scored 21 points for his country.

## ✌ RYAN'S YEAR ✌

During the 2008 RBS Six Nations Championship Ryan Jones carried the ball superbly and organized the Welsh back-row magnificently to lead his team to the Grand Slam title in his first season as captain.

## ✌ THE BIRTH OF THE IRFU ✌

The Irish Rugby Football Union was formed in 1879. Prior to 1879 Dublin University, founded in 1854, had the first organized rugby football club in Ireland. Students from the university learnt how to play rugby when they attended English public schools. Between 1874 and 1879 there were two Rugby Unions in Ireland, the Irish Football Union, which had jurisdiction over clubs in Leinster, Munster and certain parts of Ulster, and the Northern Football Union of Ireland, which controlled the Belfast-based clubs. In 1879 the two Unions agreed to amalgamate on the following terms:

(i) A Union to be known as the Irish Rugby Football
Union was to be formed for the whole country.
(ii) Branches were to be formed in Leinster, Munster and Ulster.
(iii) The Union was to be run by a Council of 18, made up of six
from each province.

*Did You Know That?*
The Connacht Branch was formed in 1886.

## ✌ FROM POLO TO RUGBY ✌

In 1922 the Scottish Football Union (SFU) announced that it had purchased 19 acres of land at Murrayfield from the Edinburgh Polo Club. The SFU then set about raising the necessary capital to transform the grounds into an international rugby arena. The requisite monies were raised from the issue of debentures, and in 1924 the SFU changed its name to become the Scottish Rugby Union.

## ✌ WALES'S LONGEST LOSING STREAK ✌

Wales endured their longest losing streak, stretching over 10 games, from 23 November 2002, when they lost 43–17 to the All Blacks at the Millennium Stadium, Cardiff, to 23 August 2003, when England won 43–9, again at the Millennium Stadium. During the period the Welsh scored 133 points but conceded 350.

## 𝒮 THE LION KEEPERS 𝒮

Don White was the first man appointed England coach in 1969. Here is the record of each coach:

| Name | Period | Games | Won | Drew | Lost | Win % |
|------|--------|-------|-----|------|------|-------|
| Don White | Dec 1969–Apr 1971 | 11 | 3 | 1 | 7 | 27.3% |
| John Elders | Jan 1972–Mar 1974 | 16 | 6 | 1 | 9 | 37.5% |
| John Burgess | Jan–May 1975 | 6 | 1 | 0 | 5 | 16.7% |
| Peter Colston | Jan 1976–Mar 1979 | 18 | 6 | 1 | 11 | 33.3% |
| Mike Davis | Nov 1979–Mar 1982 | 16 | 10 | 2 | 4 | 62.5% |
| Dick Greenwood | Jan 1983–Apr 1985 | 17 | 4 | 2 | 11 | 23.5% |
| Martin Green | Jun 1985–Jun 1987 | 14 | 5 | 0 | 9 | 35.7% |
| Geoff Cooke | Jan 1988–Mar 1994 | 35 | 13 | 1 | 21 | 37.1% |
| Jack Rowell | Jun 1994–Jul 1997 | 29 | 21 | 0 | 8 | 72.4% |
| Sir Clive Woodward | Nov 1997–Sep 2004 | 83 | 59 | 2 | 22 | 71.1% |
| Andy Robinson | Oct 2004–Nov 2006 | 22 | 9 | 0 | 13 | 40.9% |
| Brian Ashton | Dec 2006–May 2008 | 21 | 11 | 0 | 10 | 52.4% |
| Martin Johnson | May 2008–Nov 2011 | 38 | 21 | 1 | 16 | 55.3% |
| Stuart Lancaster | Dec 2011–date | 17 | 10 | 1 | 6 | 58.8% |

### *Did You Know That?*
Although appointed England coach in May 2008, Martin Johnson was not available for the summer tour of New Zealand, starting a few weeks later. Rob Andrew was tour manager and England lost both Tests.

## 𝒮 WORN WITH PRIDE: SIX NATIONS BADGES 𝒮

These are the badges worn on the shirts of the Six Nations teams:

| Country | Emblem | Country | Emblem |
|---------|--------|---------|--------|
| England | Red rose | Italy | National flag |
| France | Cockerel | Scotland | Thistle |
| Ireland | Shamrock | Wales | Prince of Wales feathers |

## 𝒮 FIVE TOO MANY 𝒮

When Ireland played their first international match in February 1875, against England, the teams comprised 20 players per side, and the Irish team included 12 players from Leinster and 8 from Ulster. Although Munster were part of the Irish Football Union, none of their players was chosen for the national team until 1879, when the IRFU was formed. Ireland's first 15-a-side match was played in 1877.

## ✌ GRAND SLAMS (6) – WALES 1971 ✌

Welsh rugby's heyday stretched from 1965 to 1979. Players such as Gareth Edwards, Barrie John, J. P. R. Williams, Gerald and Mervyn Davies and John Dawes were among the linchpins and the first three starred in the 1971 Grand Slam decider in Paris. A 70-yard interception by Williams was finished off by Edwards for one try, while John – not a noted tackler – scored the go-ahead try and kicked a penalty, both after stopping the giant flanker Benoit Dauga from scoring his second try.

### FIVE NATIONS CHAMPIONSHIP 1971

| Team | P | W | D | L | PF | PA | Pts |
|------|---|---|---|---|----|----|-----|
| Wales | 4 | 4 | 0 | 0 | 73 | 38 | 8 |
| France | 4 | 1 | 2 | 1 | 41 | 40 | 4 |
| Ireland | 4 | 1 | 1 | 2 | 41 | 46 | 3 |
| England | 4 | 1 | 1 | 2 | 44 | 58 | 3 |
| Scotland | 4 | 0 | 0 | 4 | 47 | 64 | 0 |

### RESULTS 1971 – COACH: CLIVE ROWLANDS

| Date | Venue | Opponent | Score | Captains |
|------|-------|----------|-------|----------|
| 16 January | Cardiff | England | 22–6 | SJ Dawes |
| 6 February | Edinburgh | Wales | 19–18 | SJ Dawes |
| 13 March | Dublin | Ireland | 23–9 | SJ Dawes |
| 27 March | Paris | France | 9–5 | SJ Dawes |

### Did You Know That?

In 1969, 30-year-old Clive Rowlands succeeded David Nash to become Wales's second national coach. British Lions legend Carwyn James never coached Wales.

## ✌ WHEN COLIN PASSED CARLO ✌

Carlo Checchinato won 83 caps for Italy at lock and scored 21 tries in international matches for his country, a world record for a forward that was surpassed by Wales's Colin Charvis in 2007. Checchinato retired after the 2004 Six Nations Championship, saying: "I am proud to have made a contribution to the rise in quality in Italian rugby and I will leave behind a team in great shape with enormous potential. Looking back on my career I can say every minute with the national team has been wonderful, but if I had to pick two exceptional moments they would be the tour of Australia in 1994 and last year's World Cup."

## ❦ LAMAISON SHINES ❧

During the 2001 Six Nations Championship, Christophe Lamaison became France's leading international points scorer when he took his career tally to 369 in their game against Italy. Lamaison overtook the previous record held by Thierry Lacroix. When he retired at the end of the tournament, won by France, he had amassed a total of 37 caps, and his final career tally of 380 points for his country remains a record.

## ❦ THE BEAN BARON ❧

Tony O'Reilly, later Sir Anthony O'Reilly, made his international debut for Ireland aged just 18 as a centre against France on 22 January 1955 in a 5–3 loss at Lansdowne Road, Dublin, in the Five Nations Championship. He won his 29th and final Irish cap on 14 February 1970, a 9–3 defeat by England at Twickenham, also in the Five Nations Championship. In 1955, at 19 years of age, he became the youngest player ever to play for the British Lions when they toured South Africa (Test series drawn 2–2), and represented the Lions again in 1959, winning the Test series against Australia (2–0) and losing to New Zealand (3–1). He won 10 Lions caps in total, while his total of 38 tries for the Lions, on two tours, set a mark that has never been matched. The 38 tries consisted of a record 16 in 1955 and a new record of 22 in 1959 (including six Test match tries). In addition to his exploits in the green jersey of Ireland and the famous red jersey of the British Lions, O'Reilly also holds the record for the most appearances for the Barbarians, with a staggering 30, scoring 38 tries. In April 2008, the Dublin-based publication, *Village Magazine*, reported that O'Reilly was the sixth richest Irish citizen with a net worth estimated at US$1.8 billion. When he was the CEO of the H. J. Heinz Company the media nicknamed him "The Bean Baron".

## ❦ THE BIG BULLY ❧

In 1995 Rory Underwood, his brother Tony and his mother Annie appeared in a television advertisement for Pizza Hut alongside New Zealand legend Jonah Lomu. A few months prior to filming the commercial Lomu had famously brushed aside the two brothers during the All Blacks' 45–29 win over England at Newlands, Cape Town, in the Rugby World Cup semi-finals. This time, however, the giant Lomu did not get off as lightly, as Mrs Underwood came to the rescue of her two boys and sorted him out.

## ✌ GRAND SLAM KINGS DRAW LEVEL ✌

The 1980 Five Nations Championship was the 51st series of the tournament, the 86th including the original Home Nations Championship series. England won all four of their games to draw level with the Welsh on eight Grand Slam titles, but despite also securing their 15th Triple Crown, England still trailed the Welsh by one.

## ✌ ENGLAND CAPS BILLY WHIZZ ✌

Jason Robinson won 51 caps for England between 2001 and 2007 and scored 140 points. He also won 12 caps playing Rugby League for Great Britain. Robinson was an out-and-out flying machine who combined blistering pace with tremendous agility. Indeed, he was so fast his team-mates nicknamed him "Billy Whizz" after the lightning-quick character in the *Beano* comic.

He started out in Rugby League in 1991, playing for amateur club Hunslet Parkside, then as a professional for Hunslet RLFC, but the following year he signed for Wigan, where he stayed until he switched codes in 2000. Robinson made his Rugby Union debut for Sale Sharks against Coventry in November 2000. On 17 February 2001, he made his England debut in the Six Nations Championship as a substitute against Italy. a match England won by the record score of 80–23. By gaining his first England cap he became only the second player ever to play Rugby Union for England having first played Rugby League for Great Britain (the first was Barrie-Jon Mather in 1999). In the summer of 2001 Robinson was selected for the British & Irish Lions tour to Australia and made an immediate impact in the first Test, which the Lions won 29–13 in Brisbane, before losing the series 2–1. He was named in the Lions squad again in 2005 when they toured New Zealand (lost 3–0) and in total won five caps for the Lions, scoring 10 points. Jason played in all seven of England's World Cup games in 2003 and scored a memorable try against Australia in the final.

During the 2007 Rugby World Cup finals he celebrated his 50th cap for his country when he captained the side to a 14–9 victory in the semi-final against hosts France. In the final, which was his last ever game for England, he was substituted after 46 minutes with an injury as the reigning World Cup holders lost 15–6 to South Africa. Prior to the 2007 Rugby World Cup finals Jason had announced his retirement from the sport, as he had done previously, in September 2005, only to do a U-turn.

## ❧ WIT AND WISDOM OF RUGBY (11) ❧

"France is only two hours away – it's not the other side of the world! And they actually sell ale in France, believe it or not!"
*Gareth Thomas*

## ❧ THE FIN OF SCOTTISH RUGBY ❧

Finlay "Fin" Calder won 34 caps, mainly as a flanker, for Scotland between 1986 and 1991. His twin brother, Jim, had won 27 caps earlier in the 1980s. Finlay was a relative latecomer to international rugby, making his debut at the age of 28 in a Five Nations Championship game at Murrayfield on 17 January 1986, in which Scotland beat France 18–17. Thereafter, Finlay's presence alongside the Hastings brothers, John Jeffrey, David Sole and Derek White proved to be one of the greatest back-rows Scotland has ever had. In 1989, he proudly captained the British Lions on their tour of Australia, winning the series 2–1. After helping Scotland to the Grand Slam in 1990 and going on their subsequent tour of New Zealand, Calder announced his retirement. However, the Scotland coach, Ian McGeechan, coaxed him back to international rugby to help the Scots in the 1991 Rugby World Cup and he duly obliged. His actions said more for his loyalty to his beloved Scotland, on and off the pitch, than words could ever express. Calder will go down in history as one of Scotland's greats, a ruthless attacker of the ball who had no fear in charging down a Gary Owen. He played his final game for his country during the 1991 Rugby World Cup finals, when Scotland lost 13–6 to the All Blacks on 30 October in the third-place play-off in Cardiff.

## ❧ LITTLE BIG MAN ❧

Ireland scrum-half Peter Stringer is instantly recognizable on the field, standing just 5 ft 7 ins tall (and weighing 70 kg). Despite his lack of inches Stringer is renowned for his ability to tackle men twice his bodyweight. He won his first Ireland cap on 19 February 2000, in a 44–22 win over Scotland at Lansdowne Road, Dublin, in the Five Nations Championship.

### *Did You Know That?*
On 26 February 2006, Stringer scored the last ever try at Lansdowne Road in Ireland's 31–5 Six Nations win over Wales. The stadium was then demolished to make way for Irish rugby's new home.

## ☙ YOU'RE OFF! ❧

The first recipient of an official yellow card in an international was England's Ben Clarke, when he stamped on Ireland's Simon Geoghegan in the 63rd minute of England's 20–14 Six Nations Championship defeat at Lansdowne Road on 20 October 2001. The first yellow card ever shown in an international was during the All Blacks tour of France in 1995 when the Irish referee Gordon Black showed it to the All Blacks' Mark Cooksley after the lock punched an opponent in a match at Nancy. However, Black was later informed by officials that the yellow card system had not yet been officially introduced. The first yellow card shown during a Rugby World Cup was handed to Argentina's Roberto Grau by the New Zealand referee Paddy O'Brien in the 15th minute of their 23–18 defeat to Wales in the Millennium Stadium on 1 October 1999. Meanwhile, the first player sent off in a Rugby World Cup match was Wales's Hugh Richards, who was dismissed by Australian referee Kerry Fitzgerald in the 71st minute of their 49–6 semi-final loss to New Zealand in Brisbane on 14 June 1987.

## ☙ FRANCE'S SPANGHERO BROTHERS ❧

Walter Spanghero was a member of the French side that won the Grand Slam in 1968 and was also a part of the French team which won the Five Nations Championship in both 1967 and 1973. He earned 51 caps for France, in the second and back rows. One brother, Claude, played 33 internationals, while two others were club team-mates at Narbonne. At times, half of Narbonne's pack were Spangheros.

## ☙ FIVE NATIONS LEAD THE WAY ❧

The following table lists the all-time top five countries in terms of official international matches played (as at the end of the 2013 Six Nations Championship):

| | |
|---|---|
| France | 685 |
| England | 672 |
| Wales | 645 |
| Ireland | 630 |
| Scotland | 622 |

*Did You Know That?*
The newest member of the Six Nations Championship, Italy, has played in 228 internationals.

## ✌ GAVIN BEATEN TWICE ✌

During his international career, Scotland's Gavin Hastings twice set the world record for most points in an international match, only to see his record broken by someone else within a matter of days, or even hours. At the inaugural Rugby World Cup finals in 1987, Gavin set the world record for points scored in a game when he notched up 27 points against Romania (2 tries, 8 conversions and 1 penalty) in the Scots' 55–28 win over Romania in Carisbrook, Dunedin, on 2 June 1987. Later that afternoon, his newly acquired record was broken by Didier Camberabero of France, who scored 30 points (3 tries and 9 conversions) in their 70–12 win against Zimbabwe. At the 1995 Rugby World Cup finals Gavin scored 44 points (4 tries, 9 conversions and 2 penalties) against the Ivory Coast in the Scots' 89–0 win at Olympia Park, Rustenburg, on 26 May 1995, but later in the same competition, on 4 June, Simon Culhane scored 45 points (1 try and 20 conversions) for New Zealand in a 145–17 win over Japan, a record winning margin of victory that still stands today.

## ✌ A HALF-CENTURY OF WELSH CAPTAINS ✌

In 1930 Jack Bassett from Penarth RFC became Wales's 50th captain. He led the Welsh side nine times: W6, D1, L2. Bassett was also chosen to tour Australia and New Zealand with the British Lions in 1930 and played for the Barbarians.

## ✌ SHARED TITLES ✌

Prior to the 1994 Five Nations Championship nations equal on points shared the title. The last shared title involved France and Wales in 1988, with Wales claiming the Triple Crown. Since 1995, those nations level on points have been separated by taking into consideration the difference in match points scored for and against each team.

## ✌ HOMEWARD BOUND – HOPEFULLY ✌

Italy hope that they will soon be able to return to their Stadio Flaminio home in Rome. The *Azzurri* left the smallest stadium in the Six Nations Championship as it underwent a major refurbishment. When the work is done the capacity will be increased to around 42,000. In 2012 and 2013, Italy played in the 80,000-capacity Stadio Olimpico.

## 🎗 EPIC GAMES (8) 🎗

### 1985 – IRELAND 13, ENGLAND 10

Ireland went into the final game of their 1985 Five Nations Championship knowing that a win over England at Lansdowne Road would seal their second Triple Crown in four years. The Irish were unbeaten in the tournament, with only the French having managed to get something out of them, a 15–15 draw in Dublin four weeks earlier. The game was finely balanced at 10–10 in the final minute but Michael Kiernan's dramatic drop goal gave the Irish a memorable 13–10 win. The Irish captain, Ciaran Fitzgerald, and his troops walked proudly off the pitch to a standing ovation from the ecstatic Irish fans before collecting the Five Nations Championship trophy.

## 🎗 NIJINSKY TAKES TO THE RUGBY FIELD 🎗

England's Peter Jackson (1930–2004) scored three tries in the 1957 Five Nations Championship and helped England to their first Grand Slam since 1928. In 1959 he totally bamboozled the New Zealand opposition during the British Lions' tour, scoring 16 tries in 14 games. Such was the magnificence of his performances against the All Blacks that he was described by one journalist as "the zaniest runner of all time". Jackson was affectionately nicknamed "Nijinsky", after the legendary Russian ballet dancer Vaslav Fomich Nijinsky, in recognition of his balance, style and poise.

## 🎗 THE KING OF MUNSTER 🎗

Paul O'Connell (born in Limerick, Munster) took over the captaincy of Ireland from the injured Brian O'Driscoll in their historic match against France in the Six Nations Championship on 11 February 2007. It was the first ever rugby match played at Croke Park, Dublin (home to Gaelic sports), but *Les Bleus* spoilt the Irish party, winning 20–17. However, O'Connell and his team-mates more than made up for the disappointment in their next game at the famous stadium, 13 days later, with a 43–13 thumping of England. It was Ireland's record win over the English. Fittingly, O'Connell was awarded the Man of the Match award after the famous victory. He won his first cap for the Irish on 3 February 2002 in their 54–10 win over Wales in the Five Nations Championship at Lansdowne Road, Dublin. In 2008, O'Connell captained Munster to glory in the 2008 Heineken Cup final and the 2008–09 Celtic League title and captained the British & Irish Lions side on their 2009 tour of South Africa.

## ☙ WAR HALTS HOME INTERNATIONALS ❧

The Five Nations Championship was suspended during both World Wars. During World War 1 there was no competition 1915–20 and during World War 2 the hiatus was 1940–46.

## ☙ THE BROON FRAE TROON ❧

Gordon Brown won 30 caps for Scotland between 1969 and 1976, and as a native of Troon he was affectionately nicknamed "the Broon frae Troon". Brown came from a very sporting family, his footballing father Jock having played in goal for Clyde, Hibernian, Dundee and Kilmarnock, won the Scottish Cup with Clyde (1939) and also won one international cap for Scotland. Jock also participated in the Scottish Open at Royal Troon. Gordon's mother, meanwhile, was a capable hockey player, and his older brother, Peter, also played Rugby Union for and captained Scotland. Gordon won his first cap on 6 December 1969 in a 6–3 win over South Africa and followed this up by playing in Scotland's first game of the 1970 Five Nations Championship, an 11–9 defeat by France at Murrayfield. For their next game, against Wales at the National Stadium, Cardiff, he was dropped in favour of his brother, but in the end he replaced the injured Peter for the second half of a match that Scotland lost 18–9. In addition to his 30 caps for Scotland he also won eight caps for the British Lions, playing in their 2–1 Test series win against the All Blacks in 1971, the Lions' first and, to date, only series win in New Zealand, and was a key member of the Lions side which triumphed 3–0 in the 1974 Test series in South Africa. Brown, who died of cancer on 19 March 2001, was not only one of Scotland's greatest ever players but one of the sport's best ever locks.

*Did You Know That?*
When Gordon replaced Peter against Wales in 1970 it was the first time a brother replaced a brother in an international match. Ironically, the Scotland physio who decided Peter's calf muscle was torn, and waved the towel to signal a replacement was required, was the boys' father, Jock.

## ☙ HAPPY 50TH FOR WHITE ❧

Jason White became Scotland's captain in November 2005 and celebrated his 50th cap – also as captain – in a famous 20–16 victory over France at Murrayfield in the 2006 Six Nations Championship.

## ❧ WIT AND WISDOM OF RUGBY (12) ❧

"It takes two hours to get ready – hot bath, shave my legs and face, moisturize, put fake tan on and do my hair – which takes a bit of time."
**Gavin Henson**

## ❧ IF YOU KNOW YOUR HISTORY – 9 ❧

With France invited back in the competition after a 16-year sabbatical, the Five Nations Championship resumed in 1947, with a shared victory for England and Wales.

## ❧ THE WELSH WIMBLEDON CHAMPION ❧

The legendary Welsh full-back J. P. R. Williams was a highly talented tennis player before he decided to concentrate on rugby. In 1966 he won the Junior Men's Singles title at Wimbledon.

*Did You Know That?*
Williams is a retired consultant orthopaedic surgeon.

## ❧ THE CURSE OF THE CELTS ❧

In 2001 a Celtic nation denied England the coveted Grand Slam title for the third consecutive year when Ireland beat their visitors 20–14 at Lansdowne Road (Scotland beat England 19–13 in 2000, after the Welsh had beaten them 32–31 in 1999). England were simply no match on the day for their powerful hosts, led superbly by their inspirational captain Keith Wood. Although Ireland's win meant that they drew level on points with England at the top of the table, the Six Nations Championship title went to England, who lifted the trophy before an ecstatic Irish audience in Dublin.

## ❧ THE FLYING FLY-HALF ❧

The legendary fly-half Cliff Morgan was named the greatest Welsh player of the 1950s by the Welsh Rugby Union. In the period from 1951 to 1958 Morgan played 29 times for his country and made four appearances for the British Lions. In 1952 he helped Wales to the Five Nations Grand Slam, and was part of the famous Welsh side that defeated the All Blacks in 1953. In 1955 Morgan captained the British Lions in South Africa, a Test series which ended in a 2–2 draw.

## ℣ GRAND SLAMS (7) – SCOTLAND 1990 ℣

Scotland scored only five tries in winning the 1990 Grand Slam, one each against Ireland, Wales and England – in each game 13 points was a winning score – and two against 14-man France in a 21–0 victory. The game against England was for the Calcutta Cup, Triple Crown and Grand Slam with Will Carling's men hot favourites. Jeremy Guscott scored an early try for England, but Tony Stanger scored in the corner and three Craig Chalmers penalties, allied to outstanding defending, gave Scotland the spoils 13–7.

### FIVE NATIONS CHAMPIONSHIP 1990

| Team | P | W | D | L | PF | PA | Pts |
|------|---|---|---|---|----|----|-----|
| Scotland | 4 | 4 | 0 | 0 | 60 | 26 | 8 |
| England | 4 | 3 | 0 | 1 | 90 | 26 | 6 |
| France | 4 | 2 | 0 | 2 | 67 | 78 | 4 |
| Ireland | 4 | 1 | 0 | 3 | 36 | 75 | 2 |
| Wales | 4 | 0 | 0 | 4 | 42 | 90 | 0 |

### RESULTS 1990 – COACH: IAN McGEECHAN

| Date | Venue | Opponent | Score | Captains |
|------|-------|----------|-------|----------|
| 3 February | Dublin | Ireland | 13–10 | D Sole |
| 17 February | Edinburgh | France | 21–0 | D Sole |
| 3 March | Cardiff | Wales | 13–9 | D Sole |
| 17 March | Edinburgh | England | 13–7 | D Sole |

### Did You Know That?
On a foul day at Murrayfield, Scotland skipper David Sole led the team out against England in a slow measured march. Many experts considered this move the one that unnerved England.

## ℣ THOMAS NOTCHES UP HALF-CENTURY ℣

On 8 April 2001, Gareth Thomas became only the ninth player to win 50 caps for Wales when he played against Italy in Rome in the Lloyds TSB Six Nations Championship. Wales won the match 33–23.

### Did You Know That?
Gareth Thomas's first match as the captain of Wales was against Ireland in Dublin on 16 August 2003 in his 67th appearance for his country. In what was a warm-up match for the 2003 Rugby World Cup the Welsh lost 35–12.

## ⚔ ENGLAND THE BAD LOSERS ⚔

England visited Edinburgh on 2 April 2000 knowing that a win over the auld enemy, who had lost their previous four games in the tournament, would seal the Grand Slam title for the visitors. On a rain-soaked Murrayfield pitch the all-conquering England side simply ran out of ideas while Scotland looked a completely different team knowing that a win would guarantee them the Calcutta Cup. The man of the match was Scotland's Duncan Hodge whose try, conversion and four penalties sent England home beaten 19–13 and, although champions, minus the Triple Crown and the coveted Grand Slam. After the final whistle Clive Woodward's team were booed by the home fans for not reappearing to lift the Six Nations trophy. After heavy criticism in the press the England team were later forced to issue an apology for their poor sportsmanship.

## ⚔ GIFTED BROTHERS ⚔

Brothers Kevin and Mick O'Flanagan represented Ireland at both soccer and Rugby Union. Kevin was a noted sprinter and long jumper as well as a Gaelic footballer in his early days. He then played soccer for Bohemians and Arsenal and Rugby Union for University College, Dublin, and London Irish. Kevin made 12 appearances for the Irish national soccer team between 1937 and 1947 and played for Ireland's Rugby Union side three times between 1942 and 1947. Mick, the younger brother, played for Bohemians and once for the Irish national soccer team. He also made one appearance for the Irish Rugby Union side. On 28 February 1948, he played in Ireland's 6–0 win over Scotland at Lansdowne Road, Dublin, in the Five Nations Championship (Ireland won the Grand Slam in 1948).

## ⚔ O'GARA ON THE BALL ⚔

Ronan O'Gara set a new Irish Six Nations Championship points-scoring record on 4 March 2000 when he notched 30 points (six penalties and six conversions) against Italy during a 60–13 win in Dublin.

## ⚔ THE SCOTTISH BOILER HOUSE ⚔

Gordon Brown (30 caps, 1969–76) and Alastair McHarg (44 caps, 1968–79) formed Scotland's boiler house during the 1970s. Indeed, the no-nonsense pair helped the Scots to two victories over England on consecutive Saturdays.

# ❧ FANTASY TEAMS – WALES XV ❧

**1**
Denzil
*WILLIAMS*

**2**
Bryn
*MEREDITH*

**3**
Graham
*PRICE*

**4**
Delme
*THOMAS*

**5**
Geoff
*WHEEL*

**6**
Dai
*MORRIS*

**7**
John
*TAYLOR*

**8**
Mervyn
*DAVIES*

**9**
Gareth
*EDWARDS*

**10**
Barry
*JOHN*

**11**
J. J.
*WILLIAMS*

**12**
Bleddyn
*WILLIAMS*

**13**
John
*DAWES*
*(capt)*

**14**
Gerald
*DAVIES*

**15**
J. P. R.
*WILLIAMS*

*Replacements*

16 Ieuan *EVANS* ❖ 17 Phil *BENNETT* ❖ 18 Gareth *LLEWELLYN*
19 Colin *CHARVIS* ❖ 20 Derek *QUINNELL* 21 Charlie *FAULKNER*
22 Bobby *WINDSOR* ❖ 23 Stephen *JONES*

*Coach*

Clive *ROWLANDS*

___

***Did You Know That?***
Rowlands coached Wales to the Five Nations Championship in 1969
(Triple Crown winners), 1970 (shared with France) and 1971 (Grand
Slam winners). He was Wales's coach at the 1987 Rugby World Cup.

## ❧ A LION WHO WAS NEARLY A DRAGON ❧

Despite the fact that Owen Joshua Lewsey was born in England, he
could also have played for Wales as his mother is Welsh and his father
half Welsh, half English. He won his first England cap in Australia on
the 1998 tour dubbed "The Tour of Hell". By the summer of 2007,
he had won 55 England caps and scored 110 points, as well as playing
in three Tests for the British & Irish Lions in 2005. A Rugby World
Cup winner in 2003, and part of the 2007 squad, he was omitted from
Brian Ashton's 2008 Six Nations squad. Lewsey was, however, recalled
by new coach Martin Johnson for the 2008 autumn internationals.

## ✌ THE GIUSEPPE GARIBALDI TROPHY ✌

In 2007, as part of the bicentenary celebrations commemorating the birth of Giuseppe Garibaldi, the Fédération Française de Rugby and the Federazione Italiana Rugby decided to create a trophy in his honour, to be presented to the winner of the annual Six Nations Championship game between France and Italy. The trophy was designed by the former French international and professional sculptor Jean-Pierre Rives.

## ✌ WELSH AWAY DAYS JOY ✌

In winning the Grand Slam in 2005 Wales became the first nation to win a Grand Slam title after playing more games away than at home, three on the road and two at the Millennium Stadium, Cardiff. In 2008 the Welsh repeated this remarkable feat.

## ✌ IT STARTED AND ENDED IN CARDIFF ✌

David Watkins won 21 caps for Wales at fly-half between 1963 and 1967, making his debut on 19 January 1963 in a 13–6 loss to England in Cardiff in the Five Nations Championship. He played his last game for the Welsh in Cardiff on 15 April 1967, also against England in the Five Nations Championship, but in a 34–21 win. Watkins did not start playing rugby until he was 15 years old but soon found his feet, graduating from the Glan-yr-Afon school side to Wales Youth, and aged 18 he was playing for the great Newport side of the early 1960s. On the British Lions tour to New Zealand in 1966 he captained the side in two of the Tests (lost 4–0), and in one game the legendary All Black lock, Colin Meads, just laid Watkins out flat on the field. At the end of the tour the all-conquering All Blacks went to meet the pupils at a local grammar school, where one boy asked Meads why he, a 6 ft 4 in giant, would attack little Dai Watkins. Meads furrowed his brow, looked up and said, "It was bloody self-defence!" When told about this exchange, Watkins simply said, "He [Meads] just saw me as a little nuisance buzzing around the field and felt quite justified in swatting me!"

## ✌ THE FRENCH BARBARIAN ✌

The Barbarians invited Jean-Pierre Rives on two Easter tours of South Wales, and he played for them in prestigious matches against the British Lions at Twickenham and the All Blacks at Cardiff Arms Park.

# ❧ GAVIN HASTINGS – BRAVEHEART ❧

Andrew Gavin Hastings was born on 3 January 1962 in Edinburgh, Scotland. Gavin attended George Watson's College in Edinburgh and Paisley University before completing his education at Cambridge University, where he won two blues and captained the Light Blues to victory in the 1985 Varsity Match. On 18 January 1986, he was awarded his first Scotland cap for their game against France at Murrayfield in the Five Nations Championship. He made his debut alongside his younger brother, Scott, who was also winning his first cap. Gavin's international career got off to an inauspicious start when he sent the opening kick-off into touch, and France scored a try from a quickly taken line-out without a single Scot having touched the ball. But he settled into the game and kicked six penalties, a record at the time in an international, to give Scotland an 18–17 victory. Four weeks later, Gavin kicked five penalties and three conversions in a record-breaking 33–6 win over England.

In 1990, Gavin was a key member of the Scotland team that claimed only the third Grand Slam in its history. However, 12 months later Gavin suffered perhaps his greatest disappointment in the blue of Scotland when they faced "the auld enemy", England, in a 1991 Rugby World Cup semi-final match against England at Murrayfield. With the scores level at 6–6 going into the last few minutes of the game, Gavin was given the opportunity to all but seal it for the Scots. Scotland was awarded a penalty attempt directly in front of the English posts. Under any other circumstances this would have been a relatively straightforward score for Hastings, but perhaps the pressure just crept into his boot that day, as he uncharacteristically missed, and England went on to win the game.

On 18 February 1995, Gavin scored a try against France in Paris in the Five Nations to give the Scots a 6–5 win, their first on French soil since 1969. The following year Hastings switched to American football, joining the Scottish Claymores, and won the World Bowl that year with them. Many regard Gavin as not only Scotland's greatest ever full-back but also the greatest Scottish rugby player of all time. Gavin won a total of 61 caps for Scotland, 20 as captain, played in three Rugby World Cups, and is Scotland's all-time record international points scorer with 667 points, as well as the all-time record points scorer for the British Lions in Test matches with 66. He was inducted into the International Rugby Hall of Fame in 2003, and on 30 August 2007, Gavin Hastings was named chairman of the "new" Edinburgh professional rugby club.

## *Did You Know That?*
Gavin and Scott Hastings made their debuts and won their 50th caps in the same matches, both against France at Murrayfield.

# ❧ JONATHAN DAVIES – THE PRINCE OF WALES ❧

Jonathan Davies was born in Trimsaran, Carmarthenshire, on 24 October 1962. He was introduced to rugby at the local primary school, and in 1974, while a student at Gwendraeth Grammar School, the 12-year-old Davies played for the very first time at the famous home of Welsh rugby, Cardiff Arms Park (the Millennium Stadium was a quarter of a century away). He was selected to play for the West Wales Under-12s. Jonathan left school when he was 17 to become an apprentice painter and decorator, but he continued playing rugby for Trimsaran RFC. Having been rejected following a trial by Llanelli he signed for Neath in 1982 as a fly-half, and after making his 35th appearance for the side he was called up to the senior Welsh squad. Jonathan made his debut on 20 April 1985 in a 24–15 win over England at the National Stadium, Cardiff, in the Five Nations Championship, a game in which he scored a try and a drop goal to win the man of the match award. In 1988, now a Llanelli player, he was a pivotal part of Wales's success in winning the Triple Crown, but soon afterwards, with 27 caps to his name, he switched codes. Davies left Llanelli and signed for the Rugby League side Widnes for a transfer fee of £225,000. When the Chemics (as Widnes were known in those days) experienced financial difficulties in 1993 he moved to Warrington, and during his time in Rugby League he represented both Wales (nine caps) and Great Britain (ten caps(. Davies was twice named Rugby League's Players' Player of the Year. Jonathan also found himself playing in Australia in the early 1990s, for the Canterbury Bulldogs in 1991 and the North Queensland Cowboys in 1995. In 1995, after his daughter Gena was born and his wife Karen, his childhood sweetheart at Gwendraeth Grammar School, was diagnosed with cancer, the 33-year-old Davies left Australia and moved back to Wales, where he switched codes again and joined Cardiff RFC. Rugby Union was now a professional sport. In 1996 he was awarded an MBE, but sadly the following year Karen died. He played his last game for Wales on 15 March 1997, a 34–13 defeat by England in the Five Nations Championship at the National Stadium, Cardiff – ironically where it all began for him back in 1985. In total, Jonathan, a brilliantly gifted fly-half, won 32 caps for the principality between 1985 and 1997. After his playing career ended, he was much in demand to commentate on both rugby codes.

### Did You Know That?
Jonathan Davies still holds the Welsh record for drop goals with 13. His nearest challengers are Neil Jenkins (ten) and Barry John (eight).

## 🏉 WIT AND WISDOM OF RUGBY (13) 🏉

"The whole point of rugby is that it is, first and foremost, a state of mind, a spirit."
*Jean-Pierre Rives*

## 🏉 FRENCH SLAM HAT-TRICK 🏉

In 1981 France claimed their third Grand Slam title, following those of 1968 and 1977, in what was the 52nd edition of the Five Nations Championship, the 87th of the tournament including the original Home Nations Championship series.

## 🏉 LITTLE BETWEEN THEM 🏉

On 10 January 1885 the Home/Five/Six Nations Championship witnessed its first ever drawn game, when Scotland and Wales drew 0–0 at Hamilton Crescent, Glasgow. Since then 65 more matches in the competition's three guises have ended all square. Unusually, France and Ireland shared stalemates in both 2012 (17–17) and 2013 (13–13).

## 🏉 SEEING RED 🏉

In 2004 Simon Shaw became the first England player to be shown a red card in an international when he was sent off against New Zealand. However, three England players, Mike Burton, Tim Rodber and Danny Grewcock, had all been asked to leave the field of play prior to 1999, when referees began using an actual red card.

## 🏉 SCOTLAND'S RECORD HALF-BACK DUO 🏉

John Young Rutherford won 42 caps for Scotland at fly-half between 1979 and 1987. During his international career he partnered Roy Laidlaw 35 times, which at the time was a world record for an international half-back pairing. Rutherford's final game for Scotland was their first game of the 1987 Rugby World Cup finals against France, but he was on the field for only a few minutes before a knee injury forced him off. Laidlaw won 47 caps between 1980 and 1988, a record at scrum-half for Scotland at the time, and was capped four times by the British Lions on their 1983 tour of New Zealand (lost 4–0). He played in 13 of the Lions' 18 games on the tour, captaining the side twice (wins over West Coast and Wairarapa Bush) and scoring two tries.

## ✌ THE WOODEN SPOON SOCIETY ✌

The Wooden Spoon Society was formed in 1983 after a number of England fans found themselves in a Dublin pub contemplating England's award of the wooden spoon in that year's Five Nations Championship. Rather than feel sorry for themselves the group decided to form a charity and appropriately named it the Wooden Spoon Society. Raising funds for disadvantaged children in the United Kingdom and Ireland, the charity still exists today, recognized as the official charity of British and Irish rugby.

*Did You Know That?*
The Wooden Spoon Society has a small administrative office in Frimley, Surrey, with over 40 supporting voluntary regional committees. It comprises 11,000 social members and has raised more than £12 million to date.

## ✌ THE MILLENNIUM STADIUM ✌

The Millennium Stadium, Cardiff, is the home of Welsh rugby and was built for the 1999 Rugby World Cup finals. It has a capacity of 72,500 and cost £130 million to construct, including its retractable roof. The first ever game at the stadium saw Wales take on the Rugby World Cup holders at the time, South Africa, in June 1999 – in front of just 27,000 fans as it had not yet been completed. Wales recorded their first ever win over the Springboks, a 29–19 victory.

*Did You Know That?*
Prior to the construction of the Millennium Stadium, Wales played their home games at Cardiff Arms Park and the National Stadium.

## ✌ THE LITTLE CORPORAL ✌

The former French captain and coach of the national team, Jacques Fouroux, was known as "The Little Corporal" – the nickname previously given to Napoleon Bonaparte.

## ✌ THE FRENCH SPRINGBOK ✌

French centre Brian Liebenberg was born and bred in South Africa but moved to France in 2000, where he joined Grenoble, later moving to Stade Français. In 2003 the 23-year-old Liebenberg became eligible for *Les Bleus*, and he was also selected for their Rugby World Cup squad.

## 🏉 FROM HOOKER TO MANICURIST 🏉

Former England hooker Brian Moore, winner of 64 caps for England from 1987 to 1995, was an absolute bulldog of a player on the field, never giving an inch and always at the heart of any argy-bargy when his team-mates needed some help. When he played for England he was a qualified solicitor, but when he retired from international rugby, he became a manicurist. "My wife opened a nail bar and in order to assist I decided I'd get qualified, which I did. Then sometimes I helped out in the shop and sometimes I didn't," explained Moore when asked by an interviewer about his new-found vocation. Moore's achievements on the field make impressive reading: two Grand Slams, a Rugby World Cup final, five British Lions caps and a Test series victory with the 1989 Lions in Australia. Today he is a rugby pundit for BBC Television and has returned to his original vocation as a solicitor.

*Did You Know That?*
Moore always played with the collar of his jersey tucked in.

## 🏉 THE RAGING BULL 🏉

Phil Vickery's rampaging style of play earned him the nickname "Raging Bull". He helped England to win the 2003 World Cup and captained his country in the 2008 Six Nations Championship.

## 🏉 THE FRENCH COCKEREL 🏉

The emblem adorning the French national jersey in Rugby Union is the cockerel. The indomitable cockerel has been of symbolic importance ever since Julius Caesar invaded Gaul in 52 BC.

## 🏉 THE MAN FROM THE HOLY LAND 🏉

Irish international Brendan Mullin was born in Jerusalem on 30 October 1963. Mullin won 55 caps for the Irish, making his debut on 10 November 1984 in a 16–9 defeat by Australia at Lansdowne Road, Dublin. In 1989 he toured Australia with the British Lions (won 2–1). He played his last international on 10 June 1995, Ireland losing 36–12 to France in Durban, South Africa, at the Rugby World Cup.

*Did You Know That?*
During his early career Mullin was nicknamed "Ecru" by his team-mates. Ecru was the name of a chic men's clothing shop in Dublin.

## ⚜ EPIC GAMES (9) ⚜

### 1990 – SCOTLAND 13, ENGLAND 7

This game at Murrayfield on Saint Patrick's Day 1990 was a winner-takes-all Five Nations showdown between Scotland and England, who had both won all three of their previous games in the tournament. This Calcutta Cup encounter was extra special because it was the first time in Five Nations history that the Grand Slam title was up for grabs for both teams. England were in fine form, having notched up impressive victories over Ireland at Twickenham (23–0), France in Paris (26–7) and Wales at Twickenham (34–6). Meanwhile, the Scots had beaten Ireland in Dublin (13–10), France at Murrayfield (21–0) and Wales in Cardiff (13–9). The game was a hard-fought, tense affair, and with the Scots trailing 7–6 the game's defining moment came when Gavin Hastings kicked deep into the England half and watched on as Tony Stanger raced over to score a Grand Slam-winning try which the Scots still talk about today.

## ⚜ CAPTAIN SCARLET ⚜

Delme Thomas won 25 caps for Wales between 1966 and 1974, making his debut on 3 December 1966 in a 14–11 defeat by Australia in Cardiff and playing his last game for the Welsh on 16 March 1974, a 16–12 loss to England at Twickenham in the Five Nations Championship. He was capped seven times by the British Lions. He also captained the Llanelli side, nicknamed the Scarlets, who famously beat the All Blacks 9–3 in 1972. Thomas is now universally regarded as one of the greatest locks ever to have played the game.

### Did You Know That?

The 1972 Llanelli side that brought the mighty All Blacks to their knees included Welsh legends such as Phil Bennett, Ray Gravell, Gareth Jenkins, Barry Llewellyn, Derek Quinnell and the mercurial J. J. Williams.

## ⚜ ITALY WIN AWAY AT LAST ⚜

In the 2007 RBS Six Nations Italy claimed their first ever away win of the tournament (they joined in 2000) when they defeated Scotland at Murrayfield, Edinburgh. It was also the first time the Italians had won two games in a Six Nations Championship, as they had beaten Wales in Rome.

## 🏉 GRAND SLAMS (8) – ENGLAND 2003 🏉

England's 42–6 demolition of Ireland to complete their first Six Nations Grand Slam led many observers to believe that the 2003 World Cup was theirs to lose – and so it proved. A narrow win over defending champions France was followed by increasingly confident disposals of Wales, Italy and Scotland. For once, England held their nerve in an away Grand Slam decider and in an irrepressible performance ran in five tries to end a very good Ireland team's dreams of a second Slam.

### SIX NATIONS CHAMPIONSHIP 2003

| Team | P | W | D | L | PF | PA | Pts |
|------|---|---|---|---|-----|-----|-----|
| England | 5 | 5 | 0 | 0 | 173 | 46 | 10 |
| Ireland | 5 | 4 | 0 | 1 | 119 | 97 | 8 |
| France | 5 | 3 | 0 | 2 | 153 | 75 | 6 |
| Scotland | 5 | 2 | 0 | 3 | 81 | 161 | 4 |
| Italy | 5 | 1 | 0 | 4 | 100 | 185 | 2 |
| Wales | 5 | 0 | 0 | 5 | 82 | 144 | 0 |

### RESULTS 2003 – COACH: CLIVE WOODWARD

| Date | Venue | Opponent | Score | Captains |
|------|-------|----------|-------|----------|
| 15 February | Twickenham | France | 25–17 | M Johnson |
| 22 February | Cardiff | Wales | 26–9 | M Johnson |
| 9 March | Twickenham | Italy | 40–5 | M Johnson |
| 22 March | Twickenham | Scotland | 40–9 | M Johnson |
| 30 March | Dublin | Ireland | 42–6 | M Johnson |

### Did You Know That?
In the first four years of the Six Nations, England crossed for 89 tries and scored 769 points, but their 2003 totals of 18 and 173 were the lowest in both categories.

## 🏉 FROM BALLET DANCER TO RUGBY STAR 🏉

In 1998 Caron produced its classic lavender cologne Pour un Homme (For a Man), and to promote it they chose a famous ballet dancer, Patrick Dupond, to represent the image of masculinity they desired to project in their advertising. Ten years later they opted to use France's Sebastien Chabal to promote Pour un Homme.

### Did You Know That?
In 2007 Paris Hilton recorded a song dedicated to Sebastien Chabal.

## ⚞ ENGLAND THE RECORD BUSTERS ⚟

The highest score in the history of the Six Nations Championship came on 17 February 2001 when England annihilated Italy 80–23 at Twickenham. Both the 80 points and 57-point margin remain records for the tournament. Jonny Wilkinson scored 35 points – a try, nine conversions and four penalties – to pass Ronan O'Gara's year-old single-game record of 30 points, which he scored for Ireland against Italy. The England team that day was: Iain Balshaw; Austin Healey, Will Greenwood, Mike Catt, Ben Cohen; Jonny Wilkinson, Matt Dawson; Jason Leonard, Dorian West, Phil Vickery, Martin Johnson (capt.), Danny Grewcock, Richard Hill, Neil Back, Lawrence Dallaglio. Replacements: Mark Regan, Trevor Woodman, Joe Worsley, Martin Corry, Kyran Bracken, Mike Tindall, Jason Robinson.

*Did You Know That?*
The half-time score in the game was England 33, Italy 23.

## ⚞ THAT PHOTOGRAPH ⚟

One of the most iconic photographs in world rugby is the one of the England prop, Fran Cotton, with his face completely covered in mud during the British Lions tour of New Zealand in 1977.

## ⚞ FLICKS, FLIPS, DROPS, POPS & REVERSES ⚟

Gregor Peter John Townsend won 82 caps (mainly at stand-off) for Scotland between 1993 and 2003, scoring 164 points. He also won British Lions caps in the 1997 Test series (won 2–1) in South Africa. A 19-year-old Townsend won his first Scottish cap on 6 March 1993, when he came on as a replacement for Craig Chalmers in their 26–12 loss to England at Twickenham in the Five Nations Championship. After being cast into the international wilderness in 2003, he was recalled to the Scottish squad by Frank Hadden in 2008. Few players possess the repertoire of passes that Gregor has in his locker, including flicks, flips, drops, pops and reverses. Without question Townsend is one of the most gifted and talented players rugby has ever seen.

*Did You Know That?*
Gregor scored a try in every game in the last ever Five Nations Championship in 1999, a feat no Scottish player had achieved since their Grand Slam success in 1925.

## 𝕒 WIT AND WISDOM OF RUGBY (14) 𝕓

"I play with a fear of letting people down. That's what motivates me."
*Jonny Wilkinson*

## 𝕒 DRUGS SHOCK CAUSES RESIGNATION 𝕓

On 24 May 1999, Lawrence Dallaglio sensationally resigned as England's Rugby Union captain following allegations by the *News of the World* newspaper that he took and dealt hard drugs, including cocaine and ecstasy. In response to the newspaper's claims the Rugby Football Union made the shock announcement at Twickenham following a three-hour meeting with the London Wasps star at a secret location in London. Dallaglio, aged 26, immediately informed the RFU that he would be withdrawing from the England squad to tour Australia during the summer. The newspaper also claimed that Dallaglio had boasted of taking drugs at a party during the British Lions' successful 1997 tour of South Africa (won 2–1 with Johnson as captain). However, despite tendering his resignation as captain, Dallaglio "categorically denied" that he had dealt in drugs.

## 𝕒 SCOTLAND'S FIRST HOME 𝕓

Some 26 years after Scotland played England in the first ever rugby international match, the Scottish Football Union purchased a piece of ground at Inverleith, Edinburgh, in 1897 for the sum of £3,800. Consequently, the SFU became the first of the Home Rugby Unions to own its own rugby ground. The new ground opened its doors for a match against Ireland in 1899, and a reporter's box and telephone office was created in 1901.

## 𝕒 ENGLAND PLAYERS BOYCOTT 𝕓

Following England's 25–6 win over Wales at the National Stadium, Cardiff, in the opening game of the 1991 Five Nations Championship, the entire England team, captained by Will Carling, boycotted the post-match press conference. This was unheard of at the time, and it was claimed that the players' action followed their agent being unable to agree a fee with the BBC for post-match interviews. However, Carling denied it was anything to do with money, citing the constant media harassment the players had been subjected to. England went on to win the Grand Slam in 1991.

## ✌ THE PRINCE OF THREE-QUARTERS ✌

Erith Gwyn Nicholls, nicknamed "the Prince of Three-quarters", won 24 caps (10 as captain) for Wales at centre between 1896 and 1906. Nicholls, who was born in Westbury-on-Severn, began his rugby career in 1893 with Cardiff Stars and was the only Welsh player in the British Isles team that toured Australia in 1899. Without question Nicholls was the outstanding Welsh player during their first golden age, captaining the side to three Triple Crowns and a famous win over the All Blacks in 1905. On 16 November 2005 Nicholls was inducted into the International Rugby Hall of Fame.

*Did You Know That?*
On Boxing Day 1949, the Gwyn Nicholls Memorial Gates were officially opened at Cardiff Arms Park by his former team-mate Rhys Gabe.

## ✌ THE WELSH DOUBLE CENTURION ✌

Gareth Thomas scored his 40th try for Wales (a record at the time) on 29 September 2007 in their Pool B loss against Fiji during the 2007 Rugby World Cup. In the match, which took place at the Stade de La Baujoire Stadium, Nantes, he made his 100th and final appearance for his country – becoming the first Welsh centurion – and captained the side. He also took his personal points haul for Wales to 200 points.

## ✌ THE ARGENTINE ITALIAN ✌

Diego Dominguez played international Rugby Union for both Argentina and Italy, winning 74 caps for the *Azzurri*. In 1986 Dominguez toured France with the Argentinian national side, but because of fly-half Hugo Porta's brilliant displays he failed to claim a regular place in the side. When the tour ended he remained in France, where he played club rugby until he moved to Milan the following year. In March 1991, having qualified to play for the *Azzurri* through having an Italian grandmother, Dominguez made his debut for Italy against France. He played for Italy in three Rugby World Cup finals tournaments, in 1991, 1995 and 1999. In 2002 he quit international rugby, only to be enticed out of retirement to play his very last game for Italy against Ireland on 22 February 2003, a Six Nations game which they lost 37–13 at the Stadio Flaminio, Rome. He is Italy's all-time leading points scorer with 983.

## ❦ A DANGEROUS GAME ❧

During the early 1900s Welsh fans in South Wales regularly invaded the pitch and often threatened to lynch the referee if the result of the match went against them. In the 1931 Five Nations Championship, won by Wales, some of the French players were found to have hidden stiletto knives in their socks. It was also discovered that some of their players had been paid at club level. As a result the French were banned from the tournament and were not invited back until after World War 2.

## ❦ SUPER FAB ❧

Fabien Pelous is the French record cap holder with 118 caps for his country from 1995 to 2007. The huge lock, standing 6 ft 6 ins tall and weighing in at 17 stones, made his international debut for France on 17 October 1995 in a 52–8 win over Romania in Tucuman, Argentina. In 2000 he was given the French captaincy by Bernard Laporte, only to lose it in 2002. He got it back in 2004, and proved his motivational qualities by leading his country to Six Nations Championship and Grand Slam glory. The following year *Les Bleus* finished runners-up to Grand Slam winners Wales, while at club level Pelous helped Toulouse to European Cup success. He missed the 2006 RBS Six Nations Championship after receiving a nine-week ban for elbowing Australian hooker Brendan Cannon during France's 26–16 win over the Wallabies in November 2006. Pelous was on course to equal Philippe Sella's record number of caps for France, 111, during the 2007 RBS Six Nations Championships, but an ankle injury forced him to miss the tournament. On 11 August 2007, he finally earned his record-equalling 111th cap against England in a 2007 Rugby World Cup warm-up match, a 21–15 win at Twickenham. A week later he broke the French record for appearances, winning his 112th cap in the follow-up game against England in Marseilles, a 22–9 victory for *Les Bleus*. His injury meant he lost the French captaincy to Raphael Ibanez for the 2007 Rugby World Cup finals, but he was named vice-captain for the tournament. Following the 2007 Rugby World Cup, Pelous announced his retirement, having won 118 caps (scoring 40 points), 42 of them as captain of his country. The evening after the 2007 Rugby World Cup final, Pelous was presented with the International Rugby Press Association Special Merit Award. Today Pelous is involved in a wine-making business which he and French international footballer, Djibril Cissé, began in 2002.

## ❧ MURRAYFIELD'S CLOCK TOWER ❧

In 1929 Sir David McGowan, a former president of the Scottish Football Union, gifted a clock tower to the Scottish Rugby Union which can still be seen at Murrayfield today. The clock tower was first located at the top of the terracing of the "Railway End", but following renovation work to Murrayfield during the early 1990s the clock tower was moved to its current location, at the back of the East Stand.

## ❧ HE WAS THE FIRST ❧

When Barrie-Jon Mather played for England against Wales (he was a replacement for the injured Jeremy Guscott) in their final Five Nations Championship game in 1999, the former Castleford Rugby League star became the first player to play for both national teams (Great Britain RL and England RU) since Rugby Union's professional era began.

## ❧ A VERY SPECIAL VENUE ❧

Croke Park, located on the north side of Dublin, has a capacity of 82,300. Apart from Gaelic Sports, football and rugby, Croke Park has also hosted American football and a hybrid of Gaelic/Australian Rules football matches. In 2003 the stadium hosted the spectacular opening and closing ceremonies of the 2003 Special Olympics World Summer Games, the first time they were held outside the United States.

## ❧ THE ITALIAN CENTURY MAKER ❧

Until the 2013 RBS Six Nations Championship Alessandro Troncon had made more Test appearances than any other player in Italian rugby history – 101, scoring 95 points. The legendary scrum-half made his debut against Spain in 1994. In 2007 he was named man of the match after scoring a try in Italy's first ever away win in the Six Nations Championship, 37–17 over Scotland. He made his 100th appearance for the *Azzurri* against Portugal in the 2007 Rugby World Cup, only the seventh player to reach that milestone, following George Gregan, Stephen Larkham, David Campese, Jason Leonard, Fabien Pelous and Philippe Sella. He remains one of Italy's most famous players.

### Did You Know That?
On 10 March 2013, prop Andrea Lo Cicero became Italy's most capped rugby player when he made his 102nd appearance. He retired from internationals after Italy's 22–15 win against Ireland on 16 March 2013.

## ✌ RED NOISE DAY ✊

Wales went into their final 2013 RBS Six Nations Championship match needing to beat England by a margin of eight points or more to retain their crown, while England would clinch the Grand Slam with any victory. The game was played one day after Red Nose Day, under the closed roof of the Millennium Stadium in Cardiff. A partisan sell-out crowd of 74,104 roared Wales on to a 30–3 victory, their biggest winning margin over England, and their first back-to-back championships since their Five Nations glory days, in 1978 and 1979.

## ✌ ENTER THE DRAGONS ✊

Two legendary Welsh players and future International Rugby Hall of Famers, Gerald Davies and Barry John, made their debuts together against Australia at Cardiff Arms Park on 3 December 1966. Davies went on to play 46 times for Wales between 1966 and 1978. After beginning his international career at centre, he was moved to the wing during Wales's 1969 tour of Australia and New Zealand. Davies scored 20 international tries for Wales and was a member of the British Lions that toured South Africa in 1968 (lost 3–0) and New Zealand in 1971 (won 2–1).

## ✌ IF YOU KNOW YOUR HISTORY – 10 ✊

France won their first shared Five Nations Championship title in 1954, and claimed their first outright title success in 1959.

## ✌ JEAN-PIERRE LUX ✊

Jean-Pierre Lux was capped 47 times by France between 1967 and 1975, scoring 42 points. Lux, who played at centre and on the wing, won the Five Nations Grand Slam with the French in 1968.

## ✌ IRELAND'S HARD MAN ✊

Patrick Stephen Johns, better known as Paddy Johns, won 59 caps for Ireland between 1990 and 2000. A formidable lock, Johns was as tough as nails and had a reputation on the field to match it. He made his Irish debut on 27 October 1990 in a 20–19 win over Argentina at Lansdowne Road, Dublin, and won his last cap on 11 November 2000, when Ireland thrashed Japan 78–9 in Dublin.

## ♚ WIT AND WISDOM OF RUGBY (15) ♚

"I think you enjoy the game more if you don't know the rules. Anyway, you're on the same wavelength as the referees."
*Jonathan Davies*

## ♚ WITH BAT AND BALL ♚

Thomas Mure Hart made four appearances for Scotland, two for the rugby XV and two for the cricket XI. His two rugby caps came in 1930, a 12–9 win over Wales and a 14–11 loss to Ireland. A cricket all-rounder, Hart played for Scotland once each in 1933 and 1934.

## ♚ FRENCH RUGBY ANTHEM ♚

"*La Marseillaise*" – originally "*Chant de guerre pour l'Armée du Rhin*" – meaning "War Song for the Army of the Rhine", was written and composed by Claude Joseph Rouget de Lisle in Strasbourg in 1792. The song became the rallying call of the French Revolution and was retitled after being sung by volunteers from Marseilles entering Paris.

## ♚ FRENCH COACHES ♚

| Name | Period |
|---|---|
| Jean Prat | 1964–68 |
| Fernand Cazenave | 1968–73 |
| Jean Desclaux | 1973–80 |
| Jacques Fouroux | 1981–90 |
| Daniel Dubroca | 1990–91 |
| Pierre Berbizier | 1991–95 |
| Jean-Claude Skrela | 1995–99 |
| Bernard Laporte | 1999–2007 |
| Marc Lièvremont | 2007–11 |
| Philippe Saint-André | 2011– |

## ♚ MOVE OVER BROTHER ♚

When England's Rory Underwood retired in 1996, he had won a then record 85 caps for his country, scored 49 tries (a record which still stands) and represented the British Lions on six occasions. In 1992 he was moved from England's right wing to the left wing to accommodate his younger brother Tony in the side. The duo became the first brothers to play for England at the same time since 1937.

## ✌ THE END OF AN ERA ✌

In September 2004 the Irish Minister for Arts, Sport and Tourism, John O'Donoghue, announced the redevelopment of Lansdowne Road into a 50,000-capacity all-seater stadium, due for completion in 2009. Ireland first played a Rugby Union game at Lansdowne Road on 11 March 1878, losing to England by two goals and a try to nil. Ireland's last international at the old stadium took place on 26 November 2006, when Ireland hammered the Pacific Islanders 61–17. Lansdowne Road's last ever rugby match was played on 31 December 2006 between Leinster and Ulster, the descendants of the founders of the IRFU.

### Did You Know That?
A special souvenir programme compiled by rugby historian Edmund Van Esbeck featuring great moments from the history of Lansdowne Road was sold out 15 minutes before the kick-off of the Ireland versus Pacific Islanders match.

## ✌ IRELAND'S MOST CAPPED FLY-HALF ✌

David Humphreys won 72 caps for Ireland between 1996 and 2006, scoring 560 points, and captaining the team on five occasions. In 1992, while a student at Ballymena Academy, he led the Ireland Schools side to the Schoolboys Triple Crown. Humphreys studied law at Queen's University, Belfast, and after graduating he crossed the Irish Sea to attend Oxford University. In the 1995 Varsity Match he scored all his side's points in their 21–19 loss to Cambridge (a try, a conversion, a drop goal and three penalties). Indeed, throughout his career Humphreys was an outstanding positional kicker from the hand, was an accurate and highly consistent goal-kicker and possessed exceptional speed off the mark. On 17 February 1996, he made his debut for Ireland in Paris, a 45–10 loss to the French in the Five Nations Championship. In 1999 he captained Ulster to European Cup success, and in September 2004 (versus Connacht), he became only the fourth player to win 100 caps for Ulster, joining Gary Longwell, James Topping and Andy Ward in reaching that landmark. During his career he was also capped for the Barbarians. He continued to play for Ulster until the end of the 2007–08 season, but his last game in the Irish shirt was a 31–5 win over Wales in the Five Nations Championship at Lansdowne Road, Dublin, on 26 February 2006. He retired from international rugby as Ireland's most-capped fly-half but his record has since been beaten by Ronan O'Gara.

## ✌ THE ODD SCUFFLE OR THREE ✌

Of all the nations England has played against, France and Wales in particular seem to have a special ability to light the blue touch paper, with some of England's most brutal encounters coming against these two warring nations. On 16 February 1980, England beat Wales 9–8 at Twickenham in a Five Nations Championship game which was marred by constant violence and saw Wales's Paul Ringer sent off. Ringer was handed an eight-match ban for his indiscretions, while England went on to win the Grand Slam. Seven years later, on 7 March 1987, three England players were handed bans for their part in numerous punch-ups during Wales's 19–12 victory at the National Stadium, Cardiff (known as the Battle of Cardiff). In the latter game England's Wade Dooley broke the cheekbone of Phil Davies. During England's 19–10 win over France in the quarter-finals of the 1991 Rugby World Cup at the Parc des Princes in Paris, the England players dished out some rough-house treatment to the superbly gifted Serge Blanco. It was Blanco's last ever game for his country, and he became so fed up with the treatment he was receiving that he launched an attack on Nigel Heslop, who had been nowhere near the enigmatic French winger the whole game. Twelve months later England's very own pitbull of a player, Brian Moore, got the entire French row so incensed that two of them, Grégoire Lascube and Vincent Moscato, were sent off at the Parc des Princes (where England won 31–13 *en route* to winning the Grand Slam). It was later claimed that Moscato threatened to kill Moore, an accusation Moscato denied at the time.

*Did You Know That?*
After his sending-off, Moscato never played for France again and became a boxer.


## ✌ RONAN THE FIRST ✌

On 11 February 2007, Ireland's Ronan O'Gara scored the first Irish international try at Croke Park, Dublin, when Ireland met France in the Six Nations Championship. In the same game, he became only the eighth player in history to score 800 international points. France's Raphael Ibanez scored the first ever international try at Croke Park in France's 20–17 victory.

*Did You Know That?*
O'Gara was born in San Diego, USA.

## ✇ IN THE BEGINNING ✇

The first ever rugby international match was played on the cricket field of the Edinburgh Academy at Raeburn Place, Edinburgh, on Monday 27 March 1871. Indeed, the first nine rugby international matches in Scotland were all played on established cricket fields. The Scottish Football Union commenced a search for a home ground in 1890 but experienced great difficulty in obtaining land, as many towns simply did not want an international rugby ground in their area.

## ✇ SHORT BACK AND SIDES ✇

Prior to England's famous 2003 Rugby World Cup-winning campaign their coach, Clive Woodward, made it quite clear to his players that he disliked long hair. The first player to react was Mike Catt, who, realizing that his chances of selection would be improved if he got a haircut, immediately opted for a short back and sides. Catt's reward for visiting the barber was a World Cup winner's medal.

## ✇ PRIDE OF THE PACK ✇

Jason Leonard is England's most capped player and held the world record for international caps, with 114 (scoring 5 points), until Australia's George Gregan passed his tally in 2005. Leonard won his first cap for England against Argentina in 1990 and also played 24 times (5 caps, 0 points) for the British Lions. His proudest ever moment in an England shirt was when he received a Rugby World Cup winner's medal in 2003.

## ✇ ENGLAND BECOME GRAND SLAM KINGS ✇

When England won the 1991 Five Nations Championship, Triple Crown and Grand Slam, it was their ninth Grand Slam, most among the Five Nations teams. However, they still trailed Wales in the Triple Crown table: Wales 17, England 16.

## ✇ O'GARA'S TRIPLE CROWN ✇

On 10 March 2007, Ronan O'Gara scored all of Ireland's points in their 19–18 win over Scotland at Murrayfield to win the Triple Crown. It was against Scotland at Lansdowne Road, Dublin, that O'Gara won his first cap on 19 February 2000, Ireland winning 44–22 in the Six Nations Championship.

## ⚡ SCOTT MURRAY – GIANT CONTRIBUTOR ⚡

Scott Murray was born on 15 January 1976 in Musselburgh. He went to Morgan Academy, Dundee, and Preston Lodge HS. In addition to playing rugby at school he was a Scottish Schoolboys basketball international. On a trip to his local supermarket in Prestonpans, Willie Patterson, the Preston Lodge RFC youth team coach, found the young the Murray, who grew to 6 ft 6 in and 16 st 7 lbs, stacking shelves and immediately invited him to attend a training session. Murray impressed the management at Preston Lodge and signed for the team before moving on to Edinburgh Academicals, Bedford (1996–99), Saracens (1999–2002), Edinburgh (2002–07) and French side US Montauban (from December 2007).

After playing rugby for Scotland at every youth level Murray made his A international debut against Italy in 1996, and the eighth of his nine A games saw Scotland defeat England in a 1998 A Grand Slam decider. Aged 21, he made his full international debut for Scotland on 22 November 1997 at Murrayfield in a 37–8 loss to Rugby World Cup holders, South Africa, but he did score Scotland's only try. In 1999 he was a member of the Scotland squad that famously won the last ever Five Nations Championship. In 2001 he was selected for the British Lions tour of Australia and the following year he was named the Famous Grouse Scotland Player of the Season, as he had been in 1999. A shockwave was sent around Scottish rugby in 2003 when he was sensationally left out of the squad, but he soon regained his place and first captained his country against Italy in a warm-up match they won ahead of the 2003 Rugby World Cup finals. The game also marked Murray's 50th international cap, as he became the 16th Scot to reach that landmark. The low point of his career came on 12 February 2006, when he was sent off in Scotland's 28–18 loss to Wales in the Six Nations Championship at the Millennium Stadium, Cardiff. He became only the second Scot ever to be sent off, the other being his second-row colleague Nathan Hines (against the USA Eagles on their 2002 tour).

On 10 March 2007, in a 19–18 Six Nations loss to Ireland, Murray passed Gregor Townsend to become Scotland's most capped player with 83. Murray played in three Rugby World Cups and, by the summer of 2008, had collected 87 caps, scoring 15 points. However, his Scottish caps record fell to Chris Paterson in June 2008.

### Did You Know That?

One of Murray's close friends developed the baseball video game *MLB 99*. The game contains a "cheat" in which if "Scott Murray" is typed in for a player's name, he can hit a home run a world record 700 feet.

*O*

## ✺ EPIC GAMES (10) ✺

### 1993 – WALES 10, ENGLAND 9

England went into this game as back-to-back Grand Slam winners, with just one defeat in the Five Nations Championship before that, a 13–7 loss in 1990 to Scotland (Grand Slam winners) at Murrayfield. The decisive moment of the game came just before the interval with England leading 9–3. The Welsh captain, Ieuan Evans, chipped the ball over Rory Underwood on the right wing and outran the English flying machine to the line to score. Once again the Cardiff Arms Park hoodoo sank English hearts. France claimed the Grand Slam in 1993, while the Welsh took the wooden spoon.

## ✺ THE DRAGON SLAYER ✺

On 20 March 2004, Gareth Thomas drew level with the previous record Welsh try-scorer, Ieuan Evans, when he scored his 32nd try for his country in an RBS Six Nations Championship game against England at Twickenham (Wales lost 31–21). One week later Thomas became Wales's all-time leading try-scorer when he touched down against Italy in the same tournament. It had taken Thomas eight years and ten months to pass the milestone which had stood for seven years, one month and 27 days.

## ✺ THE CHAMPAGNE SOCIALIST ✺

Richard "Dick" Spring won three caps for Ireland at full-back, his debut being against France on 20 January 1979, a 9–9 draw at Lansdowne Road, in the Five Nations Championship. His last cap came in a 12–7 Five Nations victory against England in Dublin on 17 February 1979. Spring then took up a career in politics and was first elected as a Member of the Dail for the Labour Party in 1981, retaining his seat until 2002. He was appointed party leader in 1982, and held office until 1997. During his time as the Irish Minister for Foreign Affairs (1994–97) some of his critics dubbed him a "Champagne Socialist" because during a visit to the USA he chose to stay in New York's Waldorf-Astoria Hotel rather than in the Irish-owned Fitzpatrick Hotel. In 1998, Spring played golf with US President Bill Clinton at Ballybunion Golf Club.

### Did You Know That?

Spring, born in Tralee, County Kerry, played Gaelic football and hurling for his county during the 1970s.

## ⚜ WILKINSON ON THE SILVER SCREEN ⚜

England's Jonny Wilkinson has made two DVDs: *Jonny Wilkinson: The Perfect 10* and *Jonny Wilkinson – The Real Story*. Both DVDs were released in 2003, the year he won the Rugby World Cup for England with his dramatic drop goal in the last minute of extra time against Australia in Sydney.

## ⚜ GRAND SLAM'S ROOTS ⚜

The term "Grand Slam" was first used in Rugby Union on 16 March 1957 when an article appeared in *The Times* newspaper previewing the forthcoming game between England and Scotland. The article read: "There is much more than usual at stake for England to-day in the match against Scotland at Twickenham. The last time when England achieved the Grand Slam under present conditions was as long ago as the 1927–28 season, but it is difficult to try to build up a case against her repeating the performance to-day."

***Did You Know That?***
The term Grand Slam had long been in use in the game of Contract Bridge. It is now used to describe the four major tennis tournaments: Australian Open, French Open, Wimbledon and US Open.

## ⚜ FACING APARTHEID ⚜

Mike Catt played for England from 1994 to 2007. Born in Port Elizabeth, South Africa, he toured England in 1989 with South Africa's Eastern Province side. The Springboks were banned from international competition at the time, because of the country's apartheid policy. Catt played for England at full-back, fly-half, centre and wing.

## ⚜ CROSSING THE CHANNEL ⚜

In 1996 the legendary French centre, Philippe Sella (111 caps, France 1983–95), arrived at Saracens from the French club Agen. At the time Saracens were not a big name, but it was an up-and-coming club at the time when professionalism was entering the sport. With Sella and Michael Lynagh, who also joined Saracens after retiring from a glittering 12-year international career with Australia, Saracens were soon on the way to success. Indeed, it was Sella's very presence in the side that convinced other big names in the sport to join Saracens.

## 🏉 SCOTLAND WIN ... AT LAST 🏉

On 9 February 2013, Scotland crushed Italy 34–10 at Murrayfield in the RBS Six Nations Championship. It was Scotland's first home victory in any international since a 23–12 win over Italy on 20 August 2011, a Rugby World Cup warm-up match. The Scots had not won a home match in the Six Nations Championship since beating the Italians 21–8 at Murrayfield on 19 March 2011.

## 🏉 THE SUPERSTAR 🏉

Keith Fielding made his England debut, aged 19, in a 17–15 Five Nations Championship loss to Ireland at Lansdowne Road, Dublin, on 8 February 1969. His tenth and last cap came on 18 March 1972, when England lost 23–9 at Murrayfield to Scotland. Fielding was a superfit player, as evidenced by the fact that he won the coveted BBC's *Superstars* television series title in 1981 and went on to win that year's *Superstars Challenge of Champions* title. Fielding left Rugby Union and enjoyed a long Rugby League career with Salford.

## 🏉 A SCOT OF THREE DECADES 🏉

Iain Milne won 44 caps for Scotland between 1979 and 1990. He made his debut on 3 March 1979 in an 11–11 draw with Ireland at Murrayfield in the Five Nations Championship. Milne was a durable and hard-tackling prop, who helped Scotland to Grand Slam glory in 1984. He played his last game for the Scots during their 1990 tour of New Zealand (a 21–18 loss in Auckland on 23 June 1990), but did not feature in their Grand Slam-winning team that year.

*Did You Know That?*
When Iain Milne won his 42nd cap for Scotland, his younger brother, Kenny, was winning his first at hooker.

## 🏉 A ROYAL AFFAIR 🏉

A new-look Murrayfield was opened by Princess Anne in 1994 after a redevelopment programme costing £37 million.

## 🏉 ROMAN GLADIATORS 🏉

Italy have been playing international rugby since the late 1920s and are known as the *Azzurri* (the Blues) and "the Roman Gladiators".

## &2 WIT AND WISDOM OF RUGBY (16) &2

"The time for reminiscing is after rugby. Then you can sit down and get fat."
*Josh Lewsey*

## &2 SCOTS BRING DOWN ENGLAND &2

In 1926 Scotland became the first Home Union side to defeat England at Twickenham since it opened in 1910. The English, winners of the coveted Grand Slam five times in the previous eight seasons, lost 17–9 to the Scots, who claimed the Five Nations Championship title.

## &2 A QUICK CHANGE OF RIBBONS &2

On 11 April 1999, Scott Gibbs scored the winning try in the last ever Five Nations match when Wales famously beat England 32–31 at Wembley (it was a home match for the Welsh), thereby preventing England from claiming the Grand Slam. However, just before Gibbs dramatically and sensationally won the game for the Welsh the administrators got the trophy out, put white ribbons on it and placed it on the plinth all ready to present to England. Wales's victory meant that the Five Nations title, the last ever, went to Scotland, who had beaten France 36–22 in Paris 24 hours earlier to draw level with England – and had a points difference of +41 compared with England's +25. Not for the first time, the Celtic nations had put one over on England.

## &2 TOUGH AS OLD BOOTS &2

William Patrick Duggan won 41 caps for Ireland between 1975 and 1984. He made his Irish debut on 18 January 1975 in a 12–9 win over England at Lansdowne Road, Dublin, in the Five Nations Championship. In 1977 Willie was at the peak of his powers and considered by many to be the best No. 8 in Europe at the time. He toured New Zealand the same year with the British Lions and was one of the few players the All Blacks dared not mess with. Willie was a heavy smoker with a deep dislike of training, and when his trainer once informed him that if he gave up smoking he would be faster around the pitch, Willie simply replied, "But then I would spend most of the match offside." He captained Ireland in his final international, a 32–9 loss to Scotland in Dublin on 3 March 1984.

## 🏉 GRAND SLAMS (9) – FRANCE 2004 🏉

France's eighth Grand Slam came just three months after the 2003 World Cup Final. They opened by crushing Ireland and Italy in the first two matches then, after a narrow squeak in Cardiff, they returned to dominance by blanking Scotland 31–0. In the final match World Champions England needed to win by eight points to snatch the championship. But France, courtesy of first-half Imanol Harinordoquy and Dimitri Yachvili tries and 14 points from Yachvili's boot, never trailed on their way to 24–21 victory.

### SIX NATIONS CHAMPIONSHIP 2004

| Team | P | W | D | L | PF | PA | Pts |
|------|---|---|---|---|-----|-----|-----|
| France | 5 | 5 | 0 | 0 | 144 | 60 | 10 |
| Ireland | 5 | 4 | 0 | 1 | 128 | 82 | 8 |
| England | 5 | 3 | 0 | 2 | 150 | 86 | 6 |
| Wales | 5 | 2 | 0 | 3 | 125 | 116 | 4 |
| Italy | 5 | 1 | 0 | 4 | 42 | 152 | 2 |
| Scotland | 5 | 0 | 0 | 5 | 53 | 146 | 0 |

### RESULTS 2004 – COACH: BERNARD LAPORTE

| Date | Venue | Opponent | Score | Captains |
|------|-------|----------|-------|----------|
| 14 February | Paris | Ireland | 35–17 | F Pelous |
| 21 February | Paris | Italy | 25–0 | F Pelous |
| 6 March | Cardiff | Wales | 29–22 | F Pelous |
| 6 February | Edinburgh | Scotland | 31–0 | F Pelous |
| 27 March | Paris | England | 24–21 | F Pelous |

### Did You Know That?
French captain Fabien Pelous played a record 118 times for France, 1995–2007.

## 🏉 WHEN JONNY PASSED ROB 🏉

Jonny Wilkinson's 18 points against France during the 2001 Six Nations Championship placed him on 407 international points, and ahead of Rob Andrew as England's all-time leading points scorer. He passed the 1,000 points mark in 2008.

### Did You Know That?
Jonny made his first England start on 6 June 1998 against Australia in the Cook Cup in Brisbane. The 76–0 thrashing remains England's record defeat.

## ❧ FANTASY TEAMS – FRENCH XV ❧

| | | |
|---|---|---|
| **1**<br>Gerald<br>*CHOLLY* | **2**<br>Pascal<br>*ONDARTS* | **3**<br>Robert<br>*PAPAREMBORDE* |

**4**<br>Jean-Pierre<br>*BASTIAT*   **5**<br>Fabien<br>*PELOUS*

**6**<br>Philippe<br>*SKRELA*   **7**<br>Jean-Pierre<br>*RIVES*<br>*(capt)*

**8**<br>Sebastien<br>*CHABAL*

**9**<br>Jerome<br>*GALLION*   **10**<br>Jean-Pierre<br>*ROMEUX*

**11**<br>Pierre<br>LAGISQUET   **12**<br>Philippe<br>*SELLA*   **13**<br>Yannick<br>JAUZION   **14**<br>Christophe<br>DOMINICI

**15**<br>Serge<br>*BLANCO*

### Replacements

16 Raul *IBANEZ* ❖ 17 Thierry *DUSAUTOIR* ❖ 18 Frank *MICHALAK*
19 Guy *NOVES* ❖ 20 Philippe *SAINT-ANDRE* ❖ 21 Serge *BETSEN*
22 Daniel *DUBROCA* ❖ 23 Imanol *HARINORDOQUY*

### Coach

Jacques *FOUROUX*

### Did You Know That?

Jacques Fouroux was a great leader, captaining France to Five Nations success in both 1976 and 1977, the latter year winning the Grand Slam. He was became France's coach at the age of 33 in 1981 and was in charge until 1990, a spell of 82 matches. Fouroux's France won six Five Nations titles, including two Grand Slams, reached the 1987 Rugby World Cup final and had a winning percentage of 62.19.

## ❧ WHEN MAX JOINED THE ACT ❧

In their final game of the 2005 RBS Six Nations Championship Wales, coached by Mike Ruddock, beat Ireland 32–20 at the Millennium Stadium, Cardiff, to claim their first Grand Slam since 1978. It was the first home victory for Wales over Ireland since 1983. Charlotte Church and Katherine Jenkins joined Max Boyce to sing the Welsh anthem.

By the 1970s the Five Nations Championship had become the pre-eminent international series in northern hemisphere rugby. Every match was an all-ticket event for spectators. At the same time there was also a marked increase in television interest in the tournament.

## ❧ ENGLAND RUGBY ANTHEM ❧

The exact origin of the English national anthem is uncertain. The song is believed to have been written by Henry Carey, a singer and composer, around 1736.

**God Save the Queen**
God save our gracious Queen
Long live our noble Queen,
God save the Queen:
Send her victorious,
Happy and glorious,
Long to reign over us:
God save the Queen.
O Lord, our God, arise,
Scatter thine enemies,
And make them fall:
Confound their politics,
Frustrate their knavish tricks,
On thee our hopes we fix:
God save us all.
Thy choicest gifts in store,
On her be pleased to pour;
Long may she reign:
May she defend our laws,
And ever give us cause
To sing with heart and voice
God save the Queen.

## ❧ JEFFREY PLAYS FOR WALES ❧

After Scotland were knocked out of the 1990 Hong Kong Sevens tournament, proud Scot John Jeffrey (40 caps, 1984–91), who had been playing for the Scottish side, swapped his blue shirt for the red shirt of Wales. He was permitted to play for Wales because their team was suffering from a horrendous list of injuries.

## ❦ THE POWERHOUSE ❧

In 2003 England (Grand Slam winners) claimed their third Six Nations title in four years, during which they lost only three of the 20 games they played in the competition. Amazingly, England had lost fewer games than Italy managed to win over the same period.

## ❦ LA MARSEILLAISE (SONG OF MARSEILLES) ❧

Entendez vous dans les campagnes,
Mugir ces féroces soldats?
Ils viennent jusque dans nos bras
Egorger nos fils, nos compagnes!

*Refrain (Chorus)*

Aux armes, citoyens!
Formez vos bataillons!
Marchons! Marchons!
Qu'un sang impur
Abreuve nos sillons!

Amour sacré de la patrie,
Conduis, soutiens nos bras vengeurs!
Liberté, Liberté cherie,
Combats avec tes defenseurs!
Sous nos drapeaux, que la victoire
Accoure à tes males accents!
Que tes ennemis expirants
Voient ton triomphe et notre gloire!

*Refrain*

Nous entrerons dans la carrière
Quand nos ainés n'y seront plus;
Nous y trouverons leur poussière
Et la trace de leurs vertus.
Bien moins jaloux de leur survivre
Que de partager leur cercueil,
Nous aurons le sublime orgueil
De les venger ou de les suivre!

*Refrain*

## A MAN OF MANY ADS

England's talismanic No. 10 Jonny Wilkinson has endorsed Adidas, Boots the chemist, Hackett, Lucozade and Travelex.

## THE GRAND SLAM

If a nation wins all of its games in the Six Nations Championship, then it is said to have achieved the "Grand Slam". There have been only five occasions when a nation has successfully defended the Grand Slam, i.e. achieved it again the following year: Wales in 1909, England in 1914, 1924 and 1992, and France in 1998. In 1911 Wales became the first winners of the Grand Slam in a Five Nations tournament (France were invited to join the competition in 1910), and France became the first winners of the Grand Slam in a Six Nations tournament in 2000 (the year Italy were invited to join the competition). England currently holds the record for the most Grand Slam wins with 12, followed by Wales with 11, France with 9, Scotland with 3 and Ireland with 2. Italy have yet to win more than two games in any season – or finish higher than fourth – let win alone a Grand Slam. Wales were the last Grand Slam winners in 2012.

## FINDING MY FEET

After the 2003 Rugby World Cup finals, England's Jason Robinson released his autobiography entitled *Finding My Feet: My Autobiography*.

## THE IRISH ARMY'S HOOKER

Ciaran Fitzgerald won 25 caps for Ireland at hooker from 1979 to 1986. He was already 26 years old when he made his debut for Ireland, against Australia on 3 June 1979, losing 27–12 in Brisbane. He played his final international on 15 March 1986 in a 10–9 Five Nations defeat by Scotland at Lansdowne Road. He captained Ireland to two Triple Crowns, in 1982 – their first since 1948 – and 1985, while in 1983 the Irish shared the Five Nations Championship title with France, having lost to Wales. Fitzgerald was the British Lions' captain when they toured New Zealand in 1983, the All Blacks winning 4–0. He scored only one try for his country, in a 21–7 win over Wales in Dublin in the 1980 Five Nations. Fitzgerald combined rugby with a career in the Irish army, attaining the rank of captain. He was aide-de-camp to President Dr Patrick Hillery.

## ❧ WIT AND WISDOM OF RUGBY (17) ❧

"No leadership, no ideas. Not even enough imagination to thump someone in the line-out when the ref wasn't looking."
*J. P. R. Williams* on Wales losing 28–9 against Australia

## ❧ THE CENTENARY QUAICH ❧

On 23 February 2008, Ireland beat Scotland 34–13 at Croke Park, Dublin, in the 2008 RBS Six Nations Championship. The game is significant in that Ireland won the Centenary Quaich, an award contested annually by the two nations as part of the competition. In total, Ireland and Scotland have played each other on 121 occasions, with Scotland winning 61 times, Ireland 53, with 5 games drawn. However, the trophy has only been presented to the winners of the fixture since 1989.

## ❧ ENGLAND 17, WALES 17 ❧

In 1992 England won the Five Nations Championship and the Grand Slam, their second in successive years, to draw level with Wales on 17 Triple Crown wins.

## ❧ IRISH EYES ARE SMILING ❧

In 2007 Ireland won the Triple Crown for the second year in a row and the third time in four years. France won the 2007 Six Nations Championship.

## ❧ ITALY'S LEADING TRY-SCORER ❧

Marcello Cuttitta won 54 caps for Italy and is their all-time leading try-scorer with 25.

## ❧ *STRICTLY COME DANCING* ❧

In 2006 England scrum-half Matt Dawson claimed second place in the BBC television series *Strictly Come Dancing*, partnering Lilia Kopylova. The pair lost out to England cricketer Mark Ramprakash and partner Karen Hardy. On 14 March 2008, Matt returned to the show with singer Elaine Paige in *Sport Relief Does Strictly Come Dancing*, to help raise money for Sport Relief, and once again he finished second to Ramprakash and his new partner, Kara Tointon.

## ❧ WELSH MATCH FRENCH ❧

Wales's Grand Slam win in 2012 meant that they became only the second nation after France (2002, 2004 and 2010) to win three Six Nations Championship Grand Slams. Wales won their first one in 2005 and second in 2008.

*Did You Know That?*
No nation has ever won three consecutive Grand Slams.

## ❧ JOHNSON'S GONG ❧

On 31 December 2003, it was announced that England's Rugby World Cup-winning captain, the first England player to lift the coveted Webb Ellis trophy, Martin Johnson, would receive a CBE in the 2004 New Year Honours list. He also came second to his England team-mate and fellow World Cup hero Jonny Wilkinson in the 2003 BBC Sports Personality of the Year Awards. On 17 January 2004, he confirmed his retirement from international rugby at Leicester's Heineken Cup game with Ulster and played his last game of professional rugby in Leicester's 39–14 loss to Wasps in the 2005 Zurich Grand Final. Johnson's service to England (1993–2003, 84 caps, 10 points) was further rewarded on 4 June 2005 when a Martin Johnson XV beat a Jonah Lomu XV 33–29 at Twickenham in Johnson's testimonial match, with all proceeds going to children's and cancer charities. In May 2008, he was appointed head coach of the England rugby team and resigned shortly after the 2011 Rugby World Cup.

*Did You Know That?*
Johnson had been widely tipped to replace Andy Robinson as England's head coach in November 2006, but the job went to Brian Ashton.

## ❧ A TOUCHY RULE ❧

When Wales played Scotland away during the 1963 Five Nations Championship, which was won by England, the weather conditions at Murrayfield were so horrendous that Wales's Clive Rowlands and David Watkins decided to kick into touch as often as possible. The game produced 111 line-outs, with Wales winning 6–0. After the match, the sport's governing body, the IRB, decided to introduce a rule change making it illegal for players to kick directly into touch except from within their team's own 22.

## 𝕰 EPIC GAMES (11) 𝕾

### 1995 – FRANCE 21, SCOTLAND 23

On 18 February 1995, Scotland visited the Parc des Princes to play Scotland in their second game of the 1995 Five Nations Championship. The Scots, wooden spoon winners the year before, had not beaten the French in Paris since winning 6–3 at the Stade Olympique Yves-du-Manoir, Colombes, in 1969. Scotland claimed their first ever win at the Parc des Princes thanks to a stunning last-gasp try from Gavin Hastings, who took a pass from Gregor Townsend and raced clear to score under the posts. The Scots finished second in the table to Grand Slam winners England.

## 𝕰 NOT SUCH A SMART IDEA 𝕾

Following England's 27–15 win over France at the Parc des Princes in the 1982 Five Nations Championship, the England players attended a post-match celebration dinner at the team hotel in Paris. Next to each player's place at the dinner table was a complimentary bottle of cologne. Maurice Colclough, deciding he did not require any more aftershave, emptied the flask and proceeded to refill it with wine. He then drank the flask's contents in front of his victorious team-mates. Seeing this, Colclough's team-mate Colin Smart decided he was not going to be outdone and followed suit. However, shortly after downing the flask of cologne Smart was on his way to hospital to have his stomach pumped out. "He may have been unwell," said England scrum-half Steve Smith, "but Colin had the nicest breath I've smelt."

## 𝕰 ONE-CAP WONDER FLYING MACHINE 𝕾

England's one-cap wonder, Andrew Harriman, was one of the fastest wings to have played the game. He had clocked 20.9 seconds for the 200 metres and was the primary inspiration for England's World Cup Sevens victory in 1993. He won his sole cap in England's 28–19 win over Australia in 1988, which also marked Will Carling's debut as England captain.

## 𝕰 WHEN FOUR BECAME FIVE 𝕾

During their first four years in the Five Nations Championship, from 1910 to 1913, France won just one game, a 16–15 win over Scotland in Paris in 1911.

## ❧ PLAYING BY THE NUMBERS ❧

The practice of displaying the player's number on his jersey began in 1897, when New Zealand played Queensland in Brisbane (the All Blacks' inaugural tour match). Although all international sides later followed suit during the 1930s, some nations, including the Welsh, used letters instead of numbers. During an England versus Wales game in 1939 the Welsh players wore letters on their shirts, e.g. Woller (C) and Jenkins (A).

## ❧ WHEN MARTIN OVERTOOK BILL ❧

On 16 February 2002, when England beat Ireland 45–11 at Twickenham in the Six Nations Championship, Martin Johnson captained England for the 22nd time, overtaking Bill Beaumont as his country's second most prolific captain.

## ❧ J. P. R. FOLLOWS IN GARETH'S FOOTSTEPS ❧

On 3 February 1979, J. P. R. Williams followed in the footsteps of Gareth Edwards when he became only the second Welsh player to win 50 caps for his country. Wales beat Ireland 24–21 at the Arms Park in the Five Nations Championship *en route* to winning the tournament and the Triple Crown.

*Did You Know That?*
Up until the end of May 2008, Wales had 22 players with a half-century of caps or more, of whom 12 won their 50th cap at the Millennium Stadium, Cardiff.

## ❧ PROUD BLUES ❧

Many people consider Gavin Hastings to be the greatest Scottish player of all time, while some would argue that the title should go to Andy Irvine. Both players were full-backs and they never played in the same Scottish team, Irvine's career spanning the years 1972–82 (51 caps, 273 points) while Hastings made his mark between 1986 and 1995 (61 caps and a record 67 points for his country). Both also played for the British Lions and the Barbarians.

*Did You Know That?*
Andy Irvine never once tasted victory with Scotland at Twickenham.

## 𝕺 IF YOU KNOW YOUR HISTORY – 12 𝕾

In 1972 the Five Nations Championship was not concluded, Scotland and Wales having refused to play in Dublin over security concerns.

## 𝕺 THE FUN BUS 𝕾

Jason Leonard, England prop 1990–2004, was nicknamed "the Fun Bus". Now there is a Class 357 EMU train (No. 357 003) which runs on the London, Tilbury and Southend line, servicing Jason's home town of Barking, in Essex, and bears the nameplate "Jason Leonard".

## 𝕺 A MONSTER OF A KICK 𝕾

On 1 February 1986, playing for Wales against Scotland at the Arms Park in the Five Nations Championship, Paul Thorburn kicked a penalty of world record length from inside his own half (60 metres from the posts) helping Wales to win the game 22–15. At the inaugural Rugby World Cup finals hosted jointly by New Zealand and Australia in 1987, Thorburn kicked an injury-time conversion against Australia to clinch third place, Wales's best-ever performance in the tournament. Throughout his career Thorburn was a prolific kicker, and when he retired from international rugby in 1991 he was Wales's all-time leading scorer (304 points). He also set a new record for the number of points scored in a season at Neath (438 in 1984–85), which stood for more than 20 years.

*Did You Know That?*
In 1989, Thorburn was awarded the honour of becoming the 100th Welsh team captain. He led his side 10 times between 1989 and 1991 (W1, D1, L8).

## 𝕺 ON A FOREIGN FIELD 𝕾

In seasons 1998 and 1999, while the Millennium Stadium in Cardiff was under construction, Wales played their home Five Nations Championship games at Wembley. In their "home" games of the 1998 tournament the Welsh beat Scotland 19–13 and lost 51–0 to the French (Grand Slam winners) under the old twin towers. In 1999 the Welsh lost 29–23 to the Irish at Wembley but beat England 32–31 in one of the last ever games to be played at the famous old stadium before it was demolished to make way for the new one.

# ✌ WILLIE JOHN McBRIDE – THE LION KING ✌

William James McBride was born on 6 June 1940 in Toomebridge, Northern Ireland. He attended Ballymena Academy and played for the school's First XV, but it wasn't until he was 17 years old that he started playing rugby on a regular basis. When he left school he joined Ballymena RC, and after many outstanding displays the huge lock was called up to the Irish national team. Willie made his Irish debut on 10 February 1962 at Twickenham, a 16–0 loss to England in the Five Nations Championship. Ireland won the wooden spoon in 1962, but the British Lions selectors liked what they saw and later that year included him in the Lions squad to tour South Africa.

In 1965 he was a member of the Irish side that defeated South Africa for the first time ever, a 9–6 win at Lansdowne Road on 10 April 1965. He went one better with his Irish team-mates at the Sydney Cricket Ground on 10 May 1967, when Ireland became not only the first Five Nations side to beat Australia at home, an 11–5 victory, but also the first time a Home Nations side had defeated a major southern hemisphere team in their own country. In 1966 McBride was called into the Lions squad for their tour of Australia, Canada and New Zealand, and when the Lions toured South Africa in 1968 McBride was once again an integral part of the side. By 1971 there were those who thought McBride was past his best, but the Lions coach for their tour of New Zealand, Carwyn James, knew how much a strong character like McBride was needed for the fierce battles that lay ahead against the mighty All Blacks. James made Willie his pack leader, and the powerful lock helped the Lions to claim a historic 2–1 Test series victory, their first and last series win over New Zealand. In 1974 McBride went on his fifth and final tour with the Lions, captaining the side to their first ever Test series win over South Africa.

On 15 March 1975, Willie pulled on the Irish jersey for the 63rd and final time in a 32–4 loss to Wales at Cardiff Arms Park in the Five Nations Championship. He captained Ireland 11 times and won a record 17 caps for the British Lions. McBride managed the Irish national side from 1980 to 1984, and in 1983 he was the coach of the British Lions tour of New Zealand. When the International Rugby Hall of Fame opened in 1997 he was among the inaugural inductees, and in 2004 Willie John McBride MBE was named in *Rugby World* magazine as "Heineken Rugby Personality of the Century".

### Did You Know That?
McBride scored his only try for Ireland in his penultimate international, on 1 March 1975, a 25–6 win against France in Dublin.

## 𝕰 ITALY'S BEST EVER FINISH 𝕰

In the 2007 RBS Six Nations Championship Italy finished fourth, their best ever placing since first entering the tournament in 2000.

## 𝕰 WALES'S CELTIC WARRIOR 𝕰

Neil Jenkins won 87 caps for Wales between 1991 and 2003, and along the way he etched his name in the record books once or twice for good measure. Aged just 19, he made his debut for Wales on 19 January 1991 against England in the National Stadium, Cardiff, a Five Nations game which they lost 25–6. During his early career several critics claimed he was not good enough to be in the coveted No. 10 shirt of Wales so imperiously worn by legends of the game such as Cliff Morgan, Barry John and Phil Bennett. However, Jenkins paid no attention to the criticism and went about doing what he did best, playing rugby and scoring points while setting out to improve every aspect of his game, including passing, running and tackling. Neil, nicknamed Juggie, scored 1,049 points (11 tries, 130 conversions, 235 penalties and 10 drop goals) for the principality and a further 41 points (13 penalties and a conversion) in four Tests for the British Lions. He retired from international rugby as the only player to have scored 1,000 or more points (England fly-half Jonny Wilkinson became the second in 2008). Jenkins also played fly-half at club level for Pontypridd, Cardiff and the Celtic Warriors. He played at full-back for the British Lions on their 1997 tour of South Africa, and his accuracy from goal kicks helped the Lions to a 2–1 series win over the Springboks. On the 2001 Lions tour of Australia (lost 2–1) an injury meant he only played in one of their four Tests, and his future nemesis, Jonny Wilkinson, became the preferred fly-half and goal-kicker. When he was omitted from the Welsh squad for the 2003 Rugby World Cup finals, Jenkins announced his retirement. He made his final appearance for Wales on 1 November 2002 in a 40–3 win over Romania in Wrexham. In October 2000, Jenkins was awarded an MBE, after which, rather than hang around Buckingham Palace, he jumped in a helicopter and flew back to the Welsh capital, where he scored all 24 points for Cardiff in their 24–14 win over Saracens. After hanging up his boots, Jenkins became the Welsh team's kicking coach.

### Did You Know That?

In the 2003–04 season Jenkins was successful with a world record 44 consecutive kicks at goal for his club side, the Celtic Warriors.

## ✀ WILLIAMS ALL OUT ON HIS OWN ✀

On 15 March 2008, Wales beat France 29–12 at the Millennium Stadium, Cardiff, in their final game of the 2008 RBS Six Nations Championship. When Shane Williams scored a try in the 60th minute of the game he became Wales's all-time leading try-scorer with his 41st try for his country. Wales's victory gave them their second Grand Slam title in the last four RBS Championships. Williams was playing in his 56th game for his country, and he had drawn level with the previous record-holder, Gareth Thomas, a week earlier when Wales beat Ireland 16–12 at Croke Park, Dublin. In all it took Williams eight years to reach the 40-try landmark, having scored his first international try on his second appearance for Wales, against Italy at the Millennium Stadium, Cardiff, on 19 February 2000 during the Lloyds TSB Six Nations Championship. Thomas's record had stood for just 168 days.

*Did You Know That?*
Because Wales beat France by more than three points, England finished runners-up in the table, their best RBS Six Nations finish since 2003.

## ✀ WIT AND WISDOM OF RUGBY (18) ✀

"You've got to get your first tackle in early, even if it's late."
*Ray Gravell*

## ✀ FERGUS LEADS HIS MEN DOWN UNDER ✀

John Fergus Slattery won 61 caps for Ireland, 18 as captain, between 1970 and 1984. Playing mainly at flanker he scored 12 points. Fergus made his Ireland debut on 10 January 1970 in an 8–8 draw with South Africa in Dublin. In 1971 he was called up for the British Lions tour to New Zealand but did not play in a Test match. Three years later he won three caps for the Lions on their historic winning tour of South Africa, captaining the side for two provincial matches. In 1979 Slattery captained Ireland on their tour of Australia, winning seven of eight games, including both Tests against the Wallabies – the most successful Irish touring side ever. Slattery was a key member of the Irish side that claimed the Triple Crown in 1982, their first since 1948, and made his final bow in an Irish shirt on 21 January 1984 in Paris, a 25–12 Five Nations loss to France. Fergus Slattery was inducted into the International Rugby Hall of Fame in 2007.

# ❧ THE CALCUTTA CUP ❧

On Christmas Day 1872, a game of rugby football was contested between an England XX and a XX representing Ireland, Scotland and Wales in Calcutta, India. The game marked the introduction of rugby to India, and within weeks the country's first rugby club was formed, the Calcutta Football Club. However, the new club had to wait until a second club was formed, the Calcutta Volunteers, before it could play its first game. In 1874 the Calcutta Club joined the Rugby Football Union. The Calcutta Football Club boasted several players of distinction in their membership including two England internationals, Benjamin Burns and Stephen Finney. Prior to moving to India, Burns was a banker in London who played for the Blackheath Club where he also served as secretary. In his capacity as secretary, Burns accepted a challenge issued to English clubs from the top club sides in Scotland to a match between Scotland and England. The match, the very first rugby international, proceeded and was played at Raeburn Place, Edinburgh, on 27 March 1871. The Scotland XX beat the England XX 4–1, and while Burns played in the English side he could have played in the blue of Scotland, having been educated in the country. Finney played for England against Scotland in 1872 and 1873 and was knighted in 1913. Within four years the Calcutta Football Club was forced to close through competition from other sports, most notably cricket and tennis. Upon the dissolution of the club the members had to decide what to do with the club funds, and although a grand ball was suggested, G. A. James Rothney, the club's captain, honorary secretary and treasurer, proposed that the funds be used to have a trophy made of ornate Indian workmanship and that the trophy should be offered to the Rugby Football Union in London. Upon acceptance of his idea by the members, Rothney closed the club's bank account, withdrew the entire balance due in silver rupees, and had them melted down and crafted by the finest Indian workmanship into what is now the Calcutta Cup. The stunning piece of silverware stands 18 inches high, has three handles in the shape of cobras and a lid with an elephant on top. The first ever Calcutta Cup match was played at Raeburn Place on 10 March 1879 and ended in a 3–3 draw.

### Did You Know That?
The only other time England met Scotland in a Rugby Union international match occurred during the 1991 Rugby World Cup finals, but on this occasion the Calcutta Cup was not contested. England won the game 9–6.

# 𝒪

## ❧ BBC SPORTS TEAM OF THE YEAR AWARD ☙

The BBC Sports Personality of the Year Team Award is voted for by a panel of experts, mainly former sporting superstars, towards the end of the calendar year, and is presented to the team or sporting partnership considered to have made the greatest contribution to sport in that year. It was first presented in 1960 and won by Cooper Racing. Since then rugby has featured on nine occasions:

| | |
|---|---|
| 1971 | British Lions |
| 1974 | British Lions |
| 1980 | England Rugby Union Team |
| 1990 | Scotland Rugby Union Team |
| 1991 | Joint winners: England Rugby Union Team and GB Men's Olympic 4 x 400m relay squad |
| 1993 | England Rugby Union Team |
| 1997 | British Lions |
| 2003 | England Rugby Union Team |
| 2007 | England Rugby Union Team |

## ❧ WELSH GRAND SLAM ☙

In Welsh, the Grand Slam is called *Y Gamp Lawn*. Wales were the first nation to win the Grand Slam, doing so in 1908, and have added 10 more since then (up to and including their 2012 RBS Six Nations Championship Grand Slam success).

## ❧ FORTRESS TWICKENHAM ☙

From October 1999 England enjoyed a run of 19 unbeaten home matches, ending with defeat against Ireland on 6 March 2004, when Clive Woodward coached the side.

## ❧ THE SIN BIN ☙

The sin bin is the bench where all players who have committed a yellow card offence sit out of the game for a full 10 minutes.

## ❧ DOMINANT BETWEEN THE WARS ☙

During the period between the two World Wars, England sides were the dominant force in European rugby. Their nine championship wins included five Grand Slam titles.

## ✠ WIT AND WISDOM OF RUGBY (19) ✠

"There's no such thing as lack of confidence. You either have it or you don't."
*Rob Andrew*

## ✠ ENGLAND PLAYERS THREATEN STRIKE ✠

In November 2000, England captain Martin Johnson confronted the RFU, threatening to lead the players out on strike over pay. In response the England coach, Clive Woodward, decided to issue his own counter-threat, stating that if any player failed to turn up for training before the scheduled game against Argentina that player would never play for England again. In the end a compromise deal was struck and a full England team reported for duty, but the relationships between the players, the coach and the RFU were dramatically altered.

## ✠ SMARTY PANTS ✠

Dick Greenwood, the father of Will Greenwood, a Rugby World Cup winner with England in 2003, was assistant bursar at Stonyhurst College, where he also coached rugby with Brian Ashton, and Sedbergh School. Will attended St Mary's Hall, Stonyhurst, where his mother taught mathematics until 2007. Will graduated from Hatfield College, Durham, with a BA in economics in 1984.

## ✠ L'ENIGMA ✠

When Scottish international back-row forward Simon Taylor left Edinburgh Rugby after the 2007 Rugby World Cup finals to join Stade Français in Paris, the French daily sports paper *L'Equipe* sent a reporter to the Scottish capital to write a story on the ultimate Caledonian warrior. In the course of the interview Taylor said: "I just like to keep myself to myself. I just don't have much to say about rugby. I mean there's not much to it, is there? Fifteen guys running into each other. You can analyse it all you want to, but that's what it comes down to." The interview was headlined "L'Enigma".

### *Did You Know That?*
Taylor has suffered a number of severe injuries that have resulted in him missing games. One of them was a severed toe tendon – when a dinner plate fell on his foot.

## ❧ GRAND SLAMS (10) – WALES 2008 ❧

Wales's second Grand Slam in three years came on the back of a disastrous 2007 World Cup campaign. Under new coach Warren Gatland things turned around spectacularly. The opening victory, 26–19 over England, was their first at Twickenham for 20 years. Scotland and Italy were well beaten in Cardiff before the Triple Crown was claimed in another squeaker, 16–12 in Dublin. In the finale, Shane Williams became Wales's all-time leading try-scorer with his 41st as Wales defeated France 29–12 in Cardiff.

### SIX NATIONS CHAMPIONSHIP 2008

| Team | P | W | D | L | PF | PA | Pts |
|------|---|---|---|---|-----|-----|-----|
| Wales | 5 | 5 | 0 | 0 | 148 | 66 | 10 |
| England | 5 | 3 | 0 | 2 | 108 | 83 | 6 |
| France | 5 | 3 | 0 | 2 | 103 | 93 | 6 |
| Ireland | 5 | 2 | 0 | 3 | 93 | 99 | 4 |
| Scotland | 5 | 1 | 0 | 4 | 69 | 123 | 2 |
| Italy | 5 | 1 | 0 | 4 | 74 | 131 | 2 |

### RESULTS 2008 – COACH: WARREN GATLAND

| Date | Venue | Opponent | Score | Captains |
|------|-------|----------|-------|----------|
| 2 February | Twickenham | England | 26–19 | RP Jones |
| 9 February | Cardiff | Scotland | 30–15 | RP Jones |
| 23 February | Cardiff | Italy | 47–8 | RP Jones |
| 8 March | Dublin | Ireland | 16–12 | RP Jones |
| 15 March | Cardiff | France | 29–12 | RP Jones |

### *Did You Know That?*

Between their two Grand Slams in 2005 and 2008, Wales won just two Six Nations Championship matches – 28–18 against Scotland in 2006 and 27–18 against England in 2007, both in Cardiff.

## ❧ THE ENGLISH GLADIATOR ❧

Former England centre Jeremy Guscott co-hosted the popular ITV Series *Gladiators* with Ulrika Jonsson in 1998–99.

## ❧ CAPTAIN FANTASTIC ❧

During his career Gavin Hastings captained Watsonians (in Scotland), London Scottish (in England), the Barbarians (in Hong Kong), the British Lions (in New Zealand) and Scotland (20 times).

## ◊ SCOTLAND AT HOME ◊

Scotland has played a home international Rugby Union match at the following grounds: Raeburn Place ❖ Hamilton Crescent ❖ Hampden Park ❖ Powderhall ❖ Inverleith ❖ Murrayfield.

## ◊ MR HOLLYWOOD ◊

In 1996 the England coach Jack Rowell appointed Phil de Glanville captain of the England team in succession to Will Carling. The following year England's new head coach, Clive Woodward, replaced him as captain with Lawrence Dallaglio. His team-mates often referred to Phil as "Hollywood" on account of his good looks.

*Did You Know That?*
De Glanville competed in BBC TV's 2003 *Superstars* series and won the golf and kayaking events before finishing last in the final.

## ◊ THE RAGING POTATO ◊

Keith Wood won 58 caps for Ireland at hooker between 1994 and 2003, scoring 75 points. Wood was affectionately nicknamed "the Raging Potato" because of his bald head, but was sometimes known as "Uncle Fester" after the bald character in *The Addams Family*. He made his international debut on 5 June 1994, Ireland losing 33–13 to Australia in Brisbane. Wood was a courageous player, who put his body on the line for the Irish every time he crossed the white line, and took the ball straight at the opposition. Keith played on two Lions tours, winning five caps, as the Lions defeated the mighty Springboks 2–1 in 1997 and lost 2–1 to the Wallabies in 2001. In 2001 he was the inaugural winner of the IRB World Player of the Year award, and he currently holds the world record for full international tries scored by a hooker, with 15, a record previously held by the All Blacks' Sean Fitzpatrick with 12. Woods played his last game for Ireland at the 2003 Rugby World Cup finals, captaining the side in their 43–21 loss to France in Melbourne, Australia. In 2005 he was inducted into the International Rugby Hall of Fame.

## ◊ DANNY BOY AND THE GIRLS ◊

In September 2008, new England sensation Danny Cipriani was featured in *The Observer Sport Monthly* magazine. The boyfriend of model Kelly Brook, he was photographed on the cover with three other models.

## ❧ MORGAN THE MAGNIFICENT ❧

Cliff Morgan won 29 caps for Wales between 1951 and 1958 and four Test caps for the British Lions. He made his debut for Wales on 10 March 1951 in Cardiff against Ireland in a 3–3 draw in the Five Nations Championship, with his hero, Jack Kyle, up against him. The following year Cliff helped Wales to the Grand Slam, and in 1955 he toured South Africa with the British Lions. With the Test series tied at 1–1 the Lions captain, Robin Thompson, was injured, and up stepped Morgan to skipper the side for the third Test in Pretoria. Morgan was an inspirational captain and guided the team to win 9–6, a victory that meant the Lions could not lose the series (they returned home with a highly respectable 2–2 draw with the mighty Springboks). Indeed, such was the standard of Morgan's play that the South African newspapers nicknamed him "Morgan the Magnificent" (he was also known as "the Rhondda Roundabout"). In 1956 he was appointed captain of the national side. On his retirement from the sport in 1958, Cliff joined the BBC as Sports Organizer for Wales, later becoming editor of *Sportsview* and *Grandstand*, editor of Sports Radio, Head of Outside Broadcasts for Radio and later TV. He was one of the original team captains (opposite Henry Cooper) on the popular BBC sports quiz show *A Question of Sport*.

## ❧ TEACHER TO STUDENT TO TEACHER ❧

Clive Rowlands was a teacher by profession, and played club rugby at scrum-half for Abercrave, Pontypool, Llanelli and Swansea. Amazingly, when he made his international debut for Wales against England at Cardiff Arms Park on 19 January 1963, in which Wales lost 13–6, he was made captain for the game. He retained the captaincy for the following 13 internationals, and in 1965 helped Wales to the Five Nations Championship title and their first Triple Crown since 1952. When he hung up his boots Rowlands took up coaching and managed the Welsh national team for 29 internationals between 1968 and 1974, becoming the youngest person to hold this position (he was born on 14 May 1938). He guided Wales to Five Nations Championship success in 1969 (Triple Crown winners), 1970 (shared with France) and the Grand Slam in 1971. In 1987 he managed Wales in the Rugby World Cup, and in 1989 he was manager of the British Lions tour of Australia.

*Did You Know That?*
Rowlands captained Wales in every game he played.

## ❧ WHAT A PRAT ❧

Jean Prat was awarded his first cap for France in a game against the British Army at Parc des Princes in January 1945. He got his international career off to a flying start, kicking two conversions that helped France to a 21–9 win. His first taste of Five Nations Championship encounters came in the 1947 tournament. On 9 January 1954, he captained his country for the first time when they beat Scotland 3–0 at Murrayfield in the first game of the Five Nations Championship. France ended the 1954 tournament as joint champions with England and Wales, their first ever Five Nations title. The following year the French narrowly missed out on capturing their first Grand Slam when they lost 16–11 to Wales in Colombes, which meant they shared the 1955 title with the Welsh. Prat was nicknamed "Monsieur Rugby" by the British media in recognition of his unrivalled understanding of the finer points of the game and his ability to claw a victory from a seemingly impossible situation. He led his club side Lourdes to nine championship finals, winning the French Championship six times in 10 years. Prat retired in 1955 following a game against Italy, having won 51 caps and scored 139 points for his country, including appearing on a number of occasions alongside his younger brother. Indeed, so dependable was the flank-forward that he missed only three matches of the 53 played by France following his debut. In 1964 he became the first ever coach of the French national team, and in 2001 he was inducted into the International Rugby Hall of Fame. Prat was awarded the Légion d'Honneur in 1959, the highest decoration in France.

## ❧ GRIDIRON HASTINGS ❧

In 1996 Gavin Hastings won the World Bowl with the American football team, the Scottish Claymores, at Murrayfield. However, Hastings had a disappointing season with the new ball, missing four of 27 extra point attempts and failing to score his only field goal attempt.

## ❧ A CENTURY OF CHAMPIONSHIPS ❧

The 1994 Five Nations Championship was the 65th edition under the Five Nations banner but, more importantly, the 100th of the tournament including the original Home Nations Championship series. Wales claimed the honour of winning the Centenary tournament but did not win either the Grand Slam or the Triple Crown, losing their final game 15–8 to England at Twickenham.

## ❧ MILLENNIUM TROPHY FACTS ❧

Since it was introduced in 1988, England lead the way in the Millennium Trophy with 16 wins to Ireland's ten. The biggest winning margin is 40 points which was achieved in 1997 when England won 46–6 in Dublin. The highest aggregate score of 68 points was set in 2000 when England beat Ireland 50–18 at Twickenham. In contrast the lowest-scoring game was in 2013 when Ireland lost 12–6 at the Aviva Stadium, Dublin, Owen Farrell kicking four penalties and Ronan O'Gara two. The smallest winning margin is a single point and has occurred twice, both Irish wins, 13–12 in 1994 and 14–13 in 2009. England have the longest winning run, six years, 1995–2000.

## ❧ THE FRENCH FLYING MACHINE ❧

Serge Blanco won 93 caps for France between 1980 and 1991, 81 of them at full-back and 12 on the wing, and scored 233 points for his country. He played his entire club career, 1974–92, for Biarritz Olympique. His debut for *Les Bleus* came on 8 November 1980 in a game they lost 37–15 to South Africa in Newlands. Serge is without question one of the greatest players the world has ever seen. His exciting attacking running style struck fear into even the most impenetrable of defensive walls, because no matter where on the field he picked the ball up they knew he could score from that position. Indeed, against England at Twickenham he famously began a move from behind his own try-line that resulted in a magnificent try from Philippe Saint-André in their Grand Slam decider (won 21–19 by England) on 16 March 1991. His 93rd and final game for France was on 19 October 1991, captaining the side in their 19–10 quarter-final defeat by England during the 1991 Rugby World Cup finals. When he retired he was the most capped player in the world, and today he still holds his country's try-scoring record, with 38. Serge Blanco was among the inaugural set of rugby players inducted into the International Rugby Hall of Fame in 1997.

*Did You Know That?*
Blanco was born in Caracas, the capital of Venezuela.

## ❧ THE ITALIAN WALLABY ❧

Matt Pini was born in Canberra, Australia, and was capped eight times in the No. 15 shirt for Australia, but later switched countries and became an Italian international.

## ✌ WIT AND WISDOM OF RUGBY (20) ✌

"If the game is run properly as a professional game, you do not need 57 old farts running rugby."
*Will Carling*

## ✌ THE GOLDEN BOYS ✌

Wales totally dominated the Five Nations Championship during the 1970s and ended the decade with seven championship titles (two of them shared) out of the nine tournaments played (in 1972 it was not completed), three Grand Slam titles and five Triple Crowns. The Welsh had some truly gifted rugby players during the 1970s, including their inspirational scrum-half Gareth Edwards and full-back J. P. R. Williams.

## ✌ THE ENGLISH BARON ✌

William Wavell Wakefield won 31 caps for England from 1920 to 1927 (scoring 18 points), captaining the side on 13 occasions, a record that stood until it was surpassed by Bill Beaumont (34 caps, 24 as captain, 1975–82). He made his England debut on 17 January 1920 in their 19–5 loss to Wales in Swansea in the Five Nations Championship. Wavell single-handedly revolutionized the role of the back-row forward with his exciting attacking play, which was all about piling pressure on the opposing half-backs in defence. He captained the Cambridge University team in 1922 and played 136 games for Harlequins, 82 as captain, scoring 51 tries, one penalty and 14 conversions. Wakefield, an all-round sportsman who was also an excellent cricketer, helped England to three Grand Slams in 1921, 1923 and 1924. On 2 April 1927, he played his final game for England, a 3–0 defeat to France in Paris in the Five Nations Championship. He received a knighthood in 1944, was appointed the president of the RFU in 1950, and was ennobled in 1963, becoming the first Baron Wakefield of Kendal. He also served as the president of the Ski Club of Great Britain, the British Sub Aqua Club and the British Water Ski Federation. In 1999 Sir William Wavell Wakefield was inducted as the first English member of the International Rugby Hall of Fame.

### *Did You Know That?*
Wakefield served with the Royal Flying Corps in World War 1 and was the RAF's champion over 440 yards.

## 🎬 THE CROWD PULLERS 🎬

On 1 March 1975, Scotland beat Wales 12–10 at Murrayfield in the Five Nations Championship. A crowd of 104,000 poured into the stadium, a record attendance for a northern hemisphere Rugby Union match, and third largest ever crowd at a rugby match. Only Sydney's Telstra Stadium has attracted larger attendances: 107,042 watched Australia beat New Zealand 28–7 on 28 August 1999 and 109,874 witnessed New Zealand defeat Australia 39–35 on 15 July 2000.

## 🎬 THE WELSH OLYMPIAN 🎬

Kenneth "Ken" Jeffrey Jones played 44 times for Wales and also represented the British Lions on three occasions. However, before embarking on a Rugby Union career Jones was an outstanding athlete who competed for Great Britain in the 1948 Olympic Games in London, winning a silver medal in the men's 4 x 100m relay. He also won a silver medal in the same event at the 1954 European Championships in Bern, Switzerland.

## 🎬 ASKED TO FILL BIG BOOTS 🎬

Gareth Davies, who won 21 caps for Wales between 1978 and 1985, followed in the illustrious footsteps of two legendary Welsh fly-halves, Barry John and Phil Bennett. Davies possessed superb kicking skills and could clear the ball well into the opponents' half if necessary. He made his Wales debut on 11 June 1978 in an 18–8 loss to Australia in Brisbane, and helped the Welsh to Triple Crown success in 1979. Davies was selected for the British Lions on their 1980 tour of South Africa, and won one Test cap. He played his last international on 30 March 1985 in a 14–3 loss to France in Paris.

*Did You Know That?*
In 17 of Davies's 21 Test appearances, his Cardiff club-mate Terry Holmes was at scrum-half.

## 🎬 THE MOBILE HOOKER 🎬

Brinley "Bryn" Victor Meredith was a mobile hooker who won 36 caps for Wales between 1954 and 1962 and appeared for the British Lions on eight occasions. In 1955 he was part of the Lions tour of South Africa (in which the Test series was drawn 2–2), a tour which netted Meredith a record six tries.

## ❧ EPIC GAMES (12) ❧

### 1999 – WALES 32, ENGLAND 31

With just two minutes to go on the clock, Wales trailed England in the final game of the 1999 Five Nations Championship at Wembley Stadium. England, the away team, looked poised to claim the Grand Slam, having dominated the game throughout, while Welsh fly-half Neil Jenkins had managed to keep his team in it thanks to the unerring accuracy of his kicking. With the seconds ticking by and the England players captained by Martin Johnson on the verge of thrusting their arms in the air in celebration, Scott Quinnell passed to Scott Gibbs on the England 22. The British Lions centre caught the England defence off guard and ran past six defenders to touch down next to the posts. Up stepped Jenkins, who slotted home the conversion, handing the Five Nations Championship to Scotland.

## ❧ COSY MURRAYFIELD ❧

During the summer of 1959 Murrayfield had the first ever undersoil heating system established when an "electric blanket" was laid beneath the surface. The cost of the project, £10,000, was funded by Dr C. A. Hepburn, and a plaque in recognition of his generous gift was erected at the back of the West Stand. In 1991 a new, gas-heated system of hot water pipes replaced the electric blanket.

## ❧ THE GLADIATOR ❧

Nigel Walker, who won 17 caps (scoring 12 tries) as a winger for Wales between 1993 and 1998, participated in and won the British version of the hit television series *Gladiators*.

## ❧ WHEN MATT FACED GREGOR ❧

On 9 November 2007, the 800th show of the popular BBC series *A Question of Sport* was transmitted. Former England international Matt Dawson and ex-Test cricketer Phil Tufnell were the team captains, joined by guests Gary Speed (football), Carl Fogarty (motorcycling), Ken Doherty (snooker) and Gregor Townsend (rugby).

### *Did You Know That?*

Legendary Welsh scrum-half Gareth Edwards was a captain on *A Question of Sport* from 1979 to 1981. Former Liverpool and England football skipper Emlyn Hughes was his rival captain on the show.

## ❧ THE PANTHER AND THE TIGER ❧

Prior to signing for the Leicester Tigers in 1989, England's 2003 Rugby World Cup-winning captain Martin Johnson played American football for the Leicester Panthers at both defensive end and tight end. He still enjoys the game today.

## ❧ MARATHON NUDE ❧

Matt Dawson, the former England scrum-half, completed the 2007 London marathon for charity in 4 hours, 35 minutes and 39 seconds. He also posed nude in the women's magazine *Cosmopolitan* in support of Everyman, a testicular and prostate cancer charity.

## ❧ IF YOU KNOW YOUR HISTORY – 13 ❧

Between 1910 and 1992 the winners of the Five Nations Championship did not receive a trophy. The first trophy was presented to the 1993 winners, France.

## ❧ BACK-TO-BACK FRENCH SLAMS ❧

France completed a pair of Five Nations Grand Slams in 1997 and 1998, the first time they had achieved back-to-back *Grands Chelems*.

## ❧ STADE DE FRANCE ❧

Stade de France, situated a few kilometres north of Paris in St Denis, is now the home of French rugby. It was built for the 1998 FIFA Football World Cup tournament and was the setting for the nation's greatest sporting achievement when France defeated Brazil 3–0 in the final. The impressive stadium was officially opened in January 1998, when France beat Spain 1–0 in a football international. One month later it hosted its first international rugby match, a Five Nations encounter between France and England, with the hosts winning 24–17. The Stade de France, with a capacity of 80,000, has now officially replaced the Parc des Princes as the home of French rugby. It played host to the 2007 Rugby World Cup final, in which South Africa beat England.

*Did You Know That?*
The first international try at Stade de France was scored by Philippe Bernat-Salles for France, and the first for England by Neil Back.

# ❧ FANTASY TEAMS – ITALIAN XV ❧

**1**
Andrea
*LO CICERO*

**2**
Fabio
*ONGARO*

**3**
Martin
*CASTROGIOVANNI*

**4**
Marco
*BORTOLAMI*

**5**
Santiago
*DELLAPE*

**6**
Aaron
*PERSICO*

**7**
Mauro
*BERGAMASCO*
*(capt)*

**8**
Sergio
*PARISSE*

**9**
Alessandro
*TRONCON*

**10**
Diego
*DOMINGUEZ*

**11**
Kaine
*ROBERTSON*

**12**
Christian
*STOICA*

**13**
Mirco
*BERGAMASCO*

**14**
Marcello
*CUTTITTA*

**15**
Gonzalo
*CANALE*

### Replacements
16 David *BORTOLUSSI* ❖ 17 Andrea *MASI* ❖ 18 Alessandro *ZANNI*
19 Josh *SOLE* ❖ 20 Tino *PAOLETTI* ❖ 21 Salvatore *PERUGINI*
22 Alessandro *MOSCARDI* ❖ 23 Carlo *CHECCHINATO*
### Coach
John *KIRWAN*

### Did You Know That?
John Kirwan, who scored New Zealand's final try of the inaugural World Cup Final, later played club rugby in Italy and Japan and coached both national teams.

# ❧ TOP 100 WELSH HEROES ❧

Between 8 September 2003 and 23 February 2004, Culturenet Cymru received over 80,000 nominations and votes in their quest to find the 100 Greatest Welsh Heroes of All Time. It was Wales's largest ever online poll, while the heroes featured exemplify the extraordinary talents of Welsh men and women through the ages in practically every field of human achievement. Aneurin Bevan topped the poll with 2,426 votes, while the only sportsman in the top 10 was the legendary scrum-half, Gareth Edwards, who came sixth in the poll with 1,685 votes.

## 🏉 THOMAS TAKES THE LEAD 🏉

On 26 May 2007, Gareth Thomas became Wales's most capped player when he proudly led the team out for the first Test against their hosts during their summer 2007 tour of Australia at the Telstra Stadium, Sydney. Thomas won his 93rd cap in the Test, surpassing Gareth Llewellyn's previous all-time record of 92 caps. The two sides were competing for the James Bevan Trophy for the first time. Thomas made a total of 100 appearances for Wales. Thomas was born in Bridgend on 25 July 1974. He made his debut in top-level club rugby for Bridgend against Birchgrove at the Brewery Field on 5 October 1993, playing on the wing and scoring a try in a comfortable 36–0 win.

## 🏉 THE WINNER TAKES IT ALL 🏉

In 1991 England celebrated winning their first Grand Slam title for 11 years when they beat France 21–19 in a winner-takes-all thriller at Twickenham. Both nations had won their previous three games in the tournament, and for only the second time in Five Nations history two teams faced each other for the Grand Slam on the final day (Scotland having won it in 1990 by beating England 13–7 at Murrayfield). France played superbly in the game, and scored two magnificent tries that began behind their own try-line. Legendary full-back Serge Blanco put in a mesmeric performance for *Les Bleus* in his final Five Nations appearance, but it was the more powerful England side that triumphed in the end, with Simon Hodgkinson kicking 14 points and Rory Underwood getting England's only try.

## 🏉 BROTHERS UNITED 🏉

When Gordon Brown joined his older brother Peter in the Scotland team for the first time against England in 1970, it was the first time brothers had played together for Scotland since the Bedell-Sivrights against Wales in 1902, when the Scots lost 14–5 in Cardiff to the Grand Slam winners. On 21 March 1970 the Browns helped Scotland to a 14–5 win over the auld enemy at Murrayfield in the Five Nations, helping condemn England to the wooden spoon.

### *Did You Know That?*
After Gordon Brown died in 2001, Bill McLaren said the following about the former Scottish giant of rugby: "Gordon was the type of fellow you would want as company when the shrapnel was flying."

# ॐ MIKE GIBSON – MR VERSATILITY ॐ

Cameron Michael Henderson Gibson was born on 3 December 1942 in Belfast. Mike was educated in Belfast and attended Cabin Hill Primary School and Campbell College before crossing the Irish Sea to commence a law degree at Cambridge University. While he was there he made his debut for Ireland in their 18–5 Five Nations win over England at Twickenham on 8 February 1964. In 1966, while still playing for Cambridge, he was called up for the British Lions tour of Australia, Canada and New Zealand.

Gibson was the ultimate versatile player, representing the Irish at four different positions, while the length of his international career, spanning 15 years, was a testament to his excellent fitness levels. In 1968 he embarked on his second tour with the Lions when they visited South Africa, losing 3–0 with one drawn game. Gibson possessed one of the safest pair of hands in rugby and was at his best when he broke out of the line. In his highly distinguished international career he lined up 69 times for Ireland, a record at the time, and played his last international for his beloved country aged 36, a 9–3 victory over Australia in Sydney on 16 June 1979. Gibson's fitness and love for the game saw him continue playing club rugby until he was 42 years old. In addition to his magnificent ball-handling skills he was equipped with one of the most accurate boots in the game. Gibson scored 112 international points (nine tries, 16 penalties, seven conversions and six drop goals) for Ireland. His career also saw him tour five times with the Lions, his third tour coming in 1971 in their historic 2–1 Test series win over New Zealand, the first and last time the Lions beat the mighty All Blacks. On the 1971 tour Gibson was played at fly-half and, along with Barry John and John Dawes, proved to be the catalyst for the Lions backs. In 1974 he was utilized at centre on the Lions tour of South Africa in a team captained by his fellow countryman, Willie John McBride. The Irish pair helped the Lions to a historic 3–0 Test series win (with one game drawn) over the powerful Springboks. Once again he was used at centre when the Lions toured Fiji (lost 1–0) and New Zealand (lost 3–1) in 1977. Ironically, his record total of five British Lions tours is shared with McBride.

Awarded an MBE for his services to rugby, Gibson was one of the 15 inaugural inductees to the International Rugby Hall of Fame in 1997. His record of 69 caps for the Irish stood for 26 years until it was surpassed by lock Malcolm O'Kelly against Scotland in February 2005, the same year Gibson was voted the greatest Irish international of all time.

## 🎽 FIRST WIN IN TWENTY YEARS 🎽

Wales's 26–19 win over England in the 2008 RBS Six Nations Championship was the principality's first victory against England at Twickenham in 20 years. Wales went on to clinch the Grand Slam, while England had to settle for the runners-up spot.

## 🎽 THE FAMOUS FOUR THREE-QUARTERS 🎽

Although the early Home Nations Championships were dominated by England and Scotland – between 1883 and 1892 England had three wins, Scotland two, and two were shared between them, while three tournaments were not completed – the Welsh came to the fore in 1893. Indeed, the Welsh had put together an impressive team and adopted a new system that would change the face of the game – for ever. Their famous "four three-quarters" system helped them to win all of their games in 1893 and to be crowned champions for the first time and also Triple Crown winners. The traditional system of six backs and nine forwards played by the English, Irish and Scots was simply no match for the fast, free-flowing four three-quarters system of the Welsh, which soon became the norm at both national and club level. With the new system adopted by all the Home Unions, the Irish won the title and Triple Crown for the first time the following year and repeated this success in 1896 (Home Nations winners) and 1899 (Triple Crown winners).

## 🎽 OLLY 🎽

Seamus Oliver Campbell, better known as Olly, made his Irish debut on 17 January 1976 in a 20–10 loss to Australia at Lansdowne Road, Dublin. Olly was an outstanding fly-half, and many of his greatest performances on the rugby field came while wearing the green jersey of Ireland. In 1979 he set an Irish record on Ireland's tour to Australia by scoring 60 points, 19 of them in a single match against the Wallabies – another record. On 20 February 1982, he kicked all 21 of Ireland's points in their 21–12 win over Scotland to claim the Triple Crown for the Irish, their first since 1948. He won his 22nd and final cap (having scored 217 points for Ireland) on 4 February 1984 at Lansdowne Road in a 19–18 loss to Wales in the Five Nations Championship. In addition to his Irish caps, Olly was also capped seven times by the British Lions (three times against South Africa in 1980 and four times against New Zealand in 1983), scoring 184 points for the Lions.

## ℘ THE FIVE-WAY TIE ℘

In 1973, before points difference was used as a tie-breaker, the Five Nations Championship witnessed its first and only five-way tie.

|   |          | P | W | D | L | F  | A  | Pts |
|---|----------|---|---|---|---|----|----|-----|
| 1 | Wales    | 4 | 2 | 0 | 2 | 53 | 43 | 4   |
| 1 | France   | 4 | 2 | 0 | 2 | 41 | 38 | 4   |
| 1 | Ireland  | 4 | 2 | 0 | 2 | 50 | 48 | 4   |
| 1 | Scotland | 4 | 2 | 0 | 2 | 57 | 62 | 4   |
| 1 | England  | 4 | 2 | 0 | 2 | 52 | 62 | 4   |

## ℘ A GOOD SPOT ℘

Olly Barkley was born in Hammersmith, London, but grew up in in Wadebridge, Cornwall. His talents were first spotted by England coaches Brian Ashton and Andy Robinson during the 1999–2000 season when he was playing for Colston's Collegiate School in Bristol. On 16 June 2001, he made his England debut on their tour of North America in a 48–19 win over the USA at Boxer Stadium, San Francisco, coming on as a replacement in the second half. He was only 19 years old at the time, and had not yet made a senior appearance for his club, Bath. Barkley 23 times for England (11 as a replacement) 2001–08, scoring 82 points from centre or fly-half.

## ℘ PRINCELY PARK ℘

The name Parc des Princes, "Princes' Park", dates back to the eigtheenth century when the area was a royal hunting ground. In 1897, the first Parc des Princes was opened, but it was mainly used as a velodrome and was the regular finishing point for the Tour de France. The current stadium is actually the third one – it opened in 1972 – and all were built on roughly the same site. It was the home of French rugby from 1972 to 1998, when the Stade de France opened. The Parc des Princes was used for both the 1998 FIFA and 2007 Rugby World Cups.

## ℘ WELSH MILLENNIUM MAN ℘

When Michael Owen made his debut for Wales in the first Test of the tour to South Africa on 8 June 2002, he became the 1,000th player to be capped by the Principality. The flanker had a superb debut, but Wales still lost 34–19 to their hosts at Vodacom Park, Bloemfontein.

## ❧ ITALY'S FIRST OPPONENTS ❧

In 1937 France became the first of the Five Nations teams to play Italy in an official international, which the French won 43–5.

## ❧ EARLY DAYS OF *LES BLEUS* ❧

Rugby was first played in France during the 1870s, when British merchants and students played a game in Le Havre. Its popularity quickly grew and soon students were playing the game in schools and colleges across the country. Within a few years the first clubs were formed and a club championship was founded. The first time a French national Rugby Union side played a game was at the 1900 Summer Olympics held in Paris. France beat Great Britain (represented by Mosley Wanderers RFC) 27–8 and Germany 27–17 to win the rugby gold medal. On New Year's Day 1906, France played their first ever official international, losing 38–8 to the touring All Blacks in Paris. So impressed were the visitors with the French style of play that the All Blacks' captain, Dave Gallaher, and his team-mate Billy Stead co-wrote an article in *The Complete Rugby Footballer* in which they said: "We are strongly of the opinion that the game will spread in their country and that in the course of time they will put a team in the field which will command the utmost respect of any other." The French played their first international away from home on New Year's Day 1907, losing 31–13 to England at the Athletic Ground, Richmond.

## ❧ FARMER, POLITICIAN AND PLAYER ❧

John MacDonald Bannerman, Baron Bannerman of Kildonan, OBE, was a Scottish farmer, Liberal politician and rugby player. A fiercely proud Scot, who spoke native Gaelic, won a rugby blue at Oxford University and went on to be capped 37 times by Scotland from 1921 to 1929, Bannerman later served as President of the SRU, 1954–55.

## ❧ CONFUSING THE OPPOSITION ❧

Rhys Gabe won 24 caps for Wales, 1901–08, scoring 11 tries. The most famous came against England on 18 January 1908 at a fogbound Bristol. He picked up a loose ball just outside of England's 25 and ran towards the England line. Simultaneously, team-mate Percy Bush set off in the opposite direction. Bewildered England players did not know whom to chase, but the referee did. He ran to the English posts and found a grinning Gabe with the ball at his feet. Wales won 28–18.

# *O* GRAND SLAMS (11) – IRELAND 2009

Ireland had been waiting 61 years to celebrate a Grand Slam, the second in the nation's proud history. More than 79,000 fans watched France score an early try in the opening game, before succumbing 30–21 at Croke Park. Italy were brushed aside in Rome the following week before England visited Dublin. Ronan O'Gara had an off-day, missing three of five penalty attempts, but a try and drop goal by captain fantastic Brian O'Driscoll helped Ireland to a 14–13 win. O'Gara atoned with 17 points in Ireland's 22–17 defeat of Scotland at Murrayfield to set up the decider against Wales in Cardiff. A 13-point Welsh win would snatch the championship; anything less would give Ireland the crown – but the glory of victory would be so much greater. Two Stephen Jones penalties gave Wales a 6–0 half-time lead, but two tries in two minutes, from O'Driscoll and Tommy Bowe, turned the tide. O'Gara's conversions made it 14–6, but Jones added three penalties then, with four minutes to go, dropped a goal to put Wales 15–14 up. The Irish response was immediate, with O'Gara kicking a drop goal to make it 17–15. But the drama wasn't over. Seconds from the 80-minute mark, Wales were awarded a long-range penalty. Jones's kick was off target and Ireland celebrated the Six Nations Championship, Triple Crown and Grand Slam.

## SIX NATIONS CHAMPIONSHIP 2009

| Team | P | W | D | L | PF | PA | Pts |
|------|---|---|---|---|----|----|-----|
| Ireland | 5 | 5 | 0 | 0 | 121 | 73 | 10 |
| England | 5 | 3 | 0 | 2 | 124 | 70 | 6 |
| France | 5 | 3 | 0 | 2 | 124 | 101 | 6 |
| Wales | 5 | 3 | 0 | 2 | 100 | 81 | 6 |
| Scotland | 5 | 1 | 0 | 4 | 79 | 102 | 2 |
| Italy | 5 | 0 | 0 | 5 | 49 | 170 | 0 |

## RESULTS 2009 – COACH: DECLAN KIDNEY

| Date | Venue | Opponent | Score | Captains |
|------|-------|----------|-------|----------|
| 7 February | Dublin | France | 30–21 | BG O'Driscoll |
| 15 February | Rome | Italy | 38–9 | BG O'Driscoll |
| 28 February | Dublin | England | 14–13 | BG O'Driscoll |
| 14 March | Edinburgh | Scotland | 22–15 | BG O'Driscoll |
| 21 March | Cardiff | Wales | 17–15 | BG O'Driscoll |

### *Did You Know That?*
Declan Kidney took over as team manager after Eddie O'Sullivan's resignation in the wake of Ireland's fourth-place finish in 2008.

## ❧ MORE JUDO THAN RUGBY ☙

France's 2011 Rugby World Cup captain Thierry Dusautoir had concentrated on Judo until he started playing rugby at the age of 16. The flanker, who was born in Abidjan, Côte d'Ivoire, produced numerous impressive performances in the tournament, leading France to a narrow defeat in the final to hosts New Zealand. It helped Dusautoir become only the second French player to be named IRB International Player of the Year. Fabien Galthié, who also captained France, had been the first to win the award, in 2002.

## ❧ BEWARE OF THE DOG ☙

In December 2010, former England hooker Brian Moore released his autobiography, entitled *Beware of the Dog*. The title came from his nickname, "Pitbull". Moore, who was a practising solicitor during his playing days and used to read Shakespeare in the dressing room before games, was a Grand Slam winner in 1991, 1992 and 1995. In 1991, he was named Player of the Year by *Rugby World* magazine.

## ❧ FABULOUS FABIEN ☙

Fabien Pelous won his 100th cap for France on 12 March 2005 in their 24–22 Six Nations Championship defeat of Ireland in Dublin. Only Australia's George Smith – eight years and 256 days – and Victor Matfield of South Africa – nine years and 52 days – took less time to reach the landmark than lock forward Pelous, whose 100th cap arrived nine years and 146 days after his debut.

## ❧ WALES ENTER THE FRAY ☙

Wales played their first ever international match during the 1880–81 Home Nations Championship, losing 8–0 to England at Richardson's Field, in Blackheath, London.

## ❧ SCOTLAND'S POOR RUN CONTINUES ☙

On 21 March 2009, England faced Scotland at Twickenham trying to finish runners-up in the RBS Six Nations Championship table, behind Ireland. England regained the Calcutta Cup with a 26–12 victory, which was good enough to see them finish second, ahead of France on points difference. Scotland have not won at Twickenham since 5 March 1983, though they did draw 12–12 there in 1989.

## ✌ LIGHTS GO OUT ON WALES ✌

The first ever Friday-night game in the Six Nations Championship was played at the Stade de France on 27 February 2009. France welcomed Wales, the defending RBS Six Nations Champions, who had won their opening two games. After going almost two years undefeated, Wales held high hopes of claiming their first back-to-back Grand Slams since 1909, but it was not to be: they went down 21–16. Lee Byrne's try and two penalties and a conversion from Stephen Jones had seen Wales lead 13–3 after 25 minutes, but tries from Thierry Dusautoir and Cedric Heymans, plus four more kicks from Morgan Parra turned things France's way.

## ✌ ROMAN LEADER ✌

Nick Mallett was coach of Italy from 2007 to 2011. He was born in England, but moved to Rhodesia, then South Africa as a child. Mallett played twice for the Springboks – during the Apartheid era – then became their national coach in 1997, overseeing the Boks' record 17-Test winning run, He had less success with the *Azzurri*; in fact he lost 17 times in his 20 Six Nations matches as Italy's coach, but one of those three wins came against France, 22–21, in 2011.

## ✌ BROTHERS IN GREEN ✌

After Ireland had clinched the Grand Slam, Triple Crown and RBS Six Nations Championship with their 17–15 defeat of Wales at the Millennium Stadium, Cardiff, on 15 March 2009, lock Paul O'Connell was presented with the Triple Crown trophy. Ireland's captain Brian O'Driscoll accepted the Six Nations trophy from Mary McAleese, the Irish president.

## ✌ 24–7 ✌

Scottish winger Thom Evans, who suffered a career-ending neck injury playing against Wales in 2010, used to play bass guitar and sing for a boy band called Twen2y4Se7en. Evans spent most of 2004 playing with the band, supporting acts such as Westlife and McFly.

### Did You Know That?
Thom's brother, Max, was a substitute in that match against Wales, and he scored a try in Scotland's 31–24 defeat in Cardiff. They are related to DJ and television personality Chris Evans.

## 🐾 A BAD YEAR IN BLUE 🐾

Italy endured a miserable RBS Six Nations Championship in 2009, losing all five matches, four by at least 20 points. Although they scored a respectable 49 points, they conceded 170, including 50 at home to France, 38 at home to Ireland and 36 away to England. The best result for Nick Mallett's team was a narrow 20–15 defeat against Wales in Rome. What proved to be the wooden-spoon decider, against Scotland at Murrayfield, ended in a 26–6 victory for the hosts.

## 🐾 LION OF IRELAND 🐾

Four weeks after the end of the 2009 RBS Six Nations Championship, Ireland's Paul O'Connell was appointed captain of the British & Irish Lions for their tour of South Africa. An outstanding lock and pack leader, O'Connell's leadership credentials were not in question, but he was not Ireland's captain that year. Centre Brian O'Driscoll led the team to their first Grand Slam for 61 years and was one of 14 Irishmen named in the Lions squad, but he had to return home early with an injury.

## 🐾 CAPTAIN CAVEMAN 🐾

France's back-row forward Sebastien Chabal is nicknamed *"l'homme des caverns"* (The Caveman). He became a cult hero among rugby fans during the 2007 RBS Six Nations Championship and that year's IRB World Cup as much for his flowing locks and wild beard as for his highly effective barnstorming style of play. At the end of 2012, he had played 62 times for his country and scored six tries.

## 🐾 SCOTTISH GIANT 🐾

Richard Metcalfe is not only Scotland's tallest ever player but the tallest in international rugby history. Sadly the seven-foot (2.13m) lock had a brief international career, playing only nine times between 2000 and 2001, before knee injuries forced his premature retirement.

## 🐾 WEBB MASTER 🐾

England's Jonathan Webb set the record for scoring the most points in a single Five Nations Championship, 63 in 1992. He kicked 10 conversions and eight penalties and also crossed for three tries.

## ✌ WIT AND WISDOM OF RUGBY (21) ✌

"I love the Six Nations. My interest hasn't waned in any way, shape or form over the last decade or so."
*Brian O'Driscoll, speaking in 2011*

## ✌ THE CROWD PLEASERS ✌

The 2010 RBS Six Nations Championship saw attendances top the one million mark for the first time in the history of the competition. A staggering 1,055,268 fans poured through the turnstiles to watch the 15 games, which equates to an average of 70,351 per match.

## ✌ SCOTLAND'S JOY IS ITALY'S DESPAIR ✌

Scotland's 21–9 win over Italy at Murrayfield on 19 March 2011 lifted the Scots off the foot of the table and condemned the *Azzurri* to their ninth RBS Six Nations Championship wooden spoon in their 12 seasons of playing in the competition.

## ✌ MIXED EMOTIONS IN THE ETERNAL CITY ✌

On 14 February 2010, England defeated Italy 17–12 at Rome's Stadio Flaminio, but it was a day of mixed emotions for England's legendary No. 10, Jonny Wilkinson. Although England won the game, his two missed penalties meant he went through an international without kicking a penalty for the first time since 2003.

## ✌ TON UP FOR BIG JOHN ✌

On 27 February 2010, John Hayes became the first man to make 100 international appearances for Ireland. It was a double celebration for the prop forward as he helped Ireland to 20–16 victory over England at Twickenham. His career has seen him win one Grand Slam and three Triple Crowns as well as two Heineken Cups with his province, Munster. Hayes's durability was equally legendary: not only had he been the starter in 96 of his first 99 Tests, but also he missed only 12 internationals in the 112 between his debut and century – and some of those were due to his selection for the British & Irish Lions in 2005 and 2009.

*Did You Know That?*
Hayes's 100th cap was also his 51st consecutive for Ireland.

## ⚞ WELSH MILLENNIUM MAN ⚟

When Gareth Thomas was injured during the 2005 RBS Six Nations Championship, Michael Owen was appointed captain, becoming the 122nd Welshman to lead his country. He was skipper for the last two matches, against Scotland at Murrayfield and Ireland at the Millennium Stadium, leading Wales to the nation's first Grand Slam for 27 years. More notably, when Owen made his Welsh debut in the first Test of the tour to South Africa on 8 June 2002, he became the 1,000th player to be capped by the Principality. The flanker had a superb debut, but it was in vain as Wales were beaten 34–19 at Vodacom Park, Bloemfontein.

## ⚞ WILD CHILD ⚟

Ian Smith was born in Melbourne, Australia, on 31 October 1903, and was raised in New Zealand before coming to England to study, first at Winchester School, then Brasenose College, Oxford – the same college as William Webb Ellis – where he took up rugby, having played only association football previously. Smith qualified to play for Scotland because his family came from the Borders area, though he played his club rugby for Oxford University, Edinburgh University and London Scottish. He made his international debut against Wales in the Five Nations Championship on 2 February 1924 and he scored two tries in a 35–10 Scottish win. In 1925, Smith scored four tries against France at Inverleith and four more against Wales at Swansea. He did not add to his eight tries in the Five Nations Championship that season, but his pass to Johnny Wallace resulted in the try against England which won the Grand Slam for Scotland. In his career, Smith scored 24 tries for his adopted country, a record which stood as an international record until Australia's David Campese surpassed it in 1987. Smith was a lively character and following one international at Murrayfield he went on a drinking spree which resulted in him driving his car along the pavement of Princes Street, lights blazing and horn blaring, with officers from the Edinburgh City Police Force chasing after him. When he wasn't playing rugby he practised as a solicitor.

## ⚞ THE GLADIATOR ⚟

Italy's Andrea Masi was named the 2011 RBS Six Nations Championship Player of the Tournament. The first *Azzurri* player to win the award, he received 30 per cent of the vote.

## ✸ GRAND SLAMS (12) – FRANCE 2010 ✸

After a third-place finish in the 2009 RBS Six Nations Championship, France won the Grand Slam in 2010. It was *Les Bleus'* first Grand Slam since 2004 and the third consecutive Grand Slam victory by a nation in the tournament after Wales in 2008 and Ireland in 2009. It was France's ninth overall Grand Slam victory, which includes six in the Five Nations. France had already won the Championship going into their final game with England as a result of Ireland's unexpected 23–20 home loss to the Scots just an hour before kick-off. Although England scored the only try of the game it was France who came out on top with a 12–10 victory at the Stade de France.

### SIX NATIONS CHAMPIONSHIP 2010

| Team | P | W | D | L | PF | PA | Pts |
|---|---|---|---|---|---|---|---|
| France | 5 | 5 | 0 | 0 | 135 | 69 | 10 |
| Ireland | 5 | 3 | 0 | 2 | 106 | 95 | 6 |
| England | 5 | 2 | 1 | 2 | 88 | 76 | 5 |
| Wales | 5 | 2 | 0 | 3 | 113 | 117 | 4 |
| Scotland | 5 | 1 | 1 | 3 | 83 | 100 | 3 |
| Italy | 5 | 1 | 0 | 4 | 69 | 137 | 2 |

### RESULTS 2010 – COACH: MARC LIÈVREMONT

| Date | Venue | Opponent | Score | Captains |
|---|---|---|---|---|
| 7 February | Edinburgh | Scotland | 18–9 | T Dusautoir |
| 13 February | Paris | Ireland | 33–10 | T Dusautoir |
| 26 February | Cardiff | Wales | 26–20 | T Dusautoir |
| 14 March | Paris | Italy | 46–20 | T Dusautoir |
| 20 March | Paris | England | 12–10 | T Dusautoir |

### Did You Know That?

France have claimed nine Grand Slams, six times in the Five Nations Championship and thrice in the Six Nations. Overall they have won the competition 17 times outright and shared it on eight occasions.

## ✸ SCOTLAND'S CENTENARY MAN ✸

On 13 February 2010, against Wales at the Millennium Stadium, Scotland's Chris Paterson became the 13th player to make at least 100 international appearances for his country. But it became a day to forget for him as he missed his first conversion in three years, having scored the previous 35. Although Scotland had three leads, Wales stormed back to win one of the Six Nations' most dramatic games, 31–24.

## ❧ WARBURTON'S FRENCH PAIN ☙

Sam Warburton was captain of Wales for the country's 2012 RBS Six Nations Championship Grand Slam, but lifting the trophy was a painful experience for him. He played only 160 minutes of the campaign, being hurt in the first half of the opening victory against Ireland and in the closing triumph against France – this time with a shoulder injury – and was absent altogether for the defeats of Scotland and Italy. In fact, playing against France has always been difficult for the flanker; he has not completed a full 80 minutes against *Les Bleus*.

## ❧ CALCUTTA CUP HELLO AND GOODBYE ☙

For the Calcutta Cup match on 4 March 2012, England gave seven players their international debut: Brad Barritt, Lee Dickson, Phil Dowson, Owen Farrell, Ben Morgan, Geoff Parling and Jordan Turner-Hall. Scotland had one debutant, Lee Jones, but it proved to be the last international for Dan Parks after 66 caps and 260 points.

## ❧ IRISH EYES AREN'T SMILING ☙

Ireland's 22–15 loss to Italy in the 2013 Six Nations Championship meant they finished fifth, their worst since Italy joined the competition in 2000. After the defeat in Rome, Ireland fell to ninth place in the IRB World Rankings, their lowest position since the rankings began.

## ❧ SAME OLD FACES ☙

For the first time in ten years, the 2011 Six Nations Championship saw all six nations with the same coach in place from the previous year. Although Martin Johnson (England), Marc Lièvremont (France), Declan Kidney (Ireland), Nick Mallett (Italy), Andy Robinson (Scotland) and Warren Gatland (Wales) all returned in 2011, 12 months later, however, Johnson, Lièvremont and Mallett had been replaced by Stuart Lancaster, Philippe Saint-André and Jacques Brunel, respectively.

## ❧ TAKING THE BISCUIT – TWICE ☙

On 12 March 2011, Italy beat France 22–21 at the Stadio Flaminio. Italy's first ever home win – they won at Grenoble in 1997 – meant they claimed the Giuseppe Garibaldi Trophy for the first time. Two years later, at Rome's Stadio Olimpico, Italy enjoyed a 23–18 Six Nations victory to "improve" their all-time record against France to 3–31.

## ❧ JONNY OUT IN FRONT ☙

On 26 February 2011, Jonny Wilkinson kicked a penalty goal to give England a 17–9 lead against France – it proved to be the last score of this RBS Six Nations Championship match. Those three points took Wilkinson past New Zealand's Dan Carter and made him the all-time points-scoring leader in international rugby, though Carter regained the top spot later in the year. Wilkinson retired from international rugby in December 2011, since when Ronan O'Gara of Ireland has become the leading points scorer in Six Nations Championship history.

## ❧ PLAYER CATCHES THE COACH ☙

When France defeated Italy 30–12 in Paris on 4 February 2012, Vincent Clerc scored the 32nd try of his international career, tying him with his national coach Philippe Saint-André on his country's all-time try-scoring list. Four players made their debuts in the match, Wesley Fofana and Yoann Maestri (France) and Tobias Botes and Giovanbattista Venditti (Italy).

## ❧ MOVING HOME ☙

Italy entered the Six Nations Championship in 2000 and, until 2011, played all of their home games at Rome's Stadio Flaminio. For 2012, however, Italy moved across the eternal city and played their two home games at the famous Stadio Olimpico, the stadium of two Serie A football teams, AS Roma and SS Lazio. The capacity of the Stadio Olimpico is 50 per cent larger than that of the Flaminio, accommodating 72,698 fans. The first Six Nations Championship match at Italy's new home, on 11 February 2012, attracted 53,700 fans, but England wrecked the party by winning 19–15. A month later, 72,357 watched Scotland go down 13–6 in a wooden spoon decider. This was not a national attendance record, because when New Zealand played an autumn friendly on 14 November 2009, 81,018 people were in Milan's San Siro stadium to watch the All Blacks win 20–6.

## ❧ WIT AND WISDOM OF RUGBY (22) ☙

"These boys can be regarded as being as successful as the 1970s side. Three Grand Slams since 2005 is fantastic. I think there was a mental and physical turning point in the World Cup and they have built on it."
*Jonathan Davies, former Welsh fly-half, on his country's 2012 Grand Slam*

## ❧ IRELAND'S CENTRE OF EXCELLENCE ❧

Brian O'Driscoll's father, Frank, was a pretty good player in his own right. He was good enough to be selected for the national team on two occasions, but they were Test matches for which Ireland did not award caps.

### *Did You Know That?*
Brian O'Driscoll grew up in Clotarf, the same part of Dublin as Abraham Stoker, a world champion race walker in the 1860s. Stoker changed his forename to Bram and became an author, most famously penning the story of Dracula.

## ❧ SIX NATIONS SNUBBED IN IRB AWARDS ❧

In 2001, the International Rugby Board instituted a series of awards, Player of the Year, Coach of the Year and Team of the Year. The Six Nations Championshps has been badly under-represented in these awards, collecting only 10 of the first 36. The winners are as follows:

### IRB World Player of the Year

| Year | Player | Country |
|------|--------|---------|
| 2011 | Thierry Dusautoir | France |
| 2008 | Shane Williams | Wales |
| 2003 | Jonny Wilkinson | England |
| 2002 | Fabien Galthié | France |
| 2001 | Keith Wood | Ireland |

### IRB World Coach of the Year

| Year | Coach | Country |
|------|-------|---------|
| 2009 | Declan Kidney | Ireland |
| 2003 | Clive Woodward | England |
| 2002 | Bernard Laporte | France |

### IRB World Team of the Year

| Year | Team |
|------|------|
| 2003 | England |
| 2002 | France |

## ❧ THE LIVING DAYLIGHTS ❧

For the first time since 2008, there were no Friday-night fixtures in the 2012 RBS Six Nations Championship.

## ❧ THE WOODEN SPOON WARS ❧

Between 2008 and 2012, England, France, Ireland and Wales all enjoyed victory in the RBS Six Nations Championship. Unfortunately, if you were a fan of either Italy or Scotland, any win was something to be celebrated. Neither team won more than once in any of the five seasons and they invariably battled it out for the wooden spoon. Until 2012, it was Scotland who held sway in the contest for this most unwanted prize, but their 13–6 defeat at the Stadio Olimpico in Rome on 17 March 2012 consigned the Scots not only to last place, but also their first season without a win since 2004.

## ❧ O'DRISCOLL'S LANDMARK ❧

On 13 March 2010, centre Brian O'Driscoll became only the second Irish player to make 100 appearances for his country. It was a day to remember for the captain, as he helped Ireland to a 27–12 win over Wales in the RBS Six Nations Championship at their temporary home of Croke Park in Dublin.

## ❧ ASHTON MATCHES A WAR HERO ❧

On 12 February 2011, in the RBS Six Nations Championship, England beat Italy 59–13 at Twickenham. England winger Chris Ashton scored four tries in the game, thereby becoming the first player to achieve the feat since Italy joined the competition in 2000. Ashton also became the first England player to enjoy a four-try performance in any of the tournament's guises since Ronald Poulton touched down four times against France in Paris on 13 April 1914. England, captained by Poulton, won that match 39–13 to complete the Grand Slam. Lieutenant Poulton served in the 1st/4th Royal Berkshire Regiment during the First World War but was killed by a sniper's bullet on 5 May 1915. Having scored two tries in England's defeat of Wales in the competition opener, Ashton's six tries already equalled the single season record in the Six Nations Championship era, a mark held by Will Greenwood (England) and Shane Williams (Wales). However, Ashton could not add to his tally of six in the last three matches.

## ❧ *LES BLEUS* DENY WALES CHAMPIONSHIP ❧

Wales needed a 27-point winning margin over France at the Stade de France to clinch the 2011 RBS Six Nations Championship. However, *Les Bleus* won 28–9 to give England the crown.

## ✌ GRAND SLAMS (13) – WALES 2012 ✌

Wales won the Grand Slam in nerve-jangling style after almost losing it in the first match. Only a last-minute penalty from Leigh Halfpenny gave them victory over Ireland at the Aviva Stadium, Dublin. In their third match, against England at Twickenham, the hosts had a late try ruled out by the TMO (television match official), having trailed 12–9 with eight minutes to go. This win sealed the Welsh Triple Crown. The title was almost wrapped up before France visited Cardiff in the final match, but Alex Cuthbert't try and four Halfpenny kicks ensured a fifth victory of the campaign.

### SIX NATIONS CHAMPIONSHIP 2012

| Team | P | W | D | L | PF | PA | Pts |
|------|---|---|---|---|----|----|-----|
| Wales | 5 | 5 | 0 | 0 | 109 | 58 | 10 |
| England | 5 | 4 | 0 | 1 | 98 | 71 | 8 |
| Ireland | 5 | 2 | 1 | 2 | 121 | 94 | 5 |
| France | 5 | 2 | 1 | 2 | 101 | 86 | 5 |
| Italy | 5 | 1 | 0 | 4 | 53 | 121 | 2 |
| Scotland | 5 | 0 | 0 | 5 | 56 | 108 | 0 |

### RESULTS 2012 – COACH: WARREN GATLAND

| Date | Venue | Opponent | Score | Captains |
|------|-------|----------|-------|----------|
| 5 February | Dublin | Ireland | 23–21 | S Warburton |
| 12 February | Cardiff | Scotand | 27–13 | RP Jones |
| 25 February | Twickenham | England | 19–12 | S Warburton |
| 10 March | Cardiff | Italy | 24–3 | G Jenkins |
| 17 March | Cardiff | France | 16–9 | S Warburton |

### Did You Know That?
Welsh celebrations were muted as victory over France came two days after the death of Mervyn Davies, captain of the 1976 Grand Slam team. In Davies's memory, back-row forward Ryan Jones wore a headband reminiscent of the legendary No. 8.

## ✌ THE TIMES THEY ARE A-CHANGIN' ✌

The 2013 RBS Six Nations Championship was the 14th in its current format. However, it was the 119th Northern Hemisphere Rugby Union Championship which includes the tournament's time as the Home Nations Championship (1883–1909, 1932–39) and Five Nations Championship (1910–39, 1947–99). World Wars 1 and 2 meant there were no championships 1915–19 and 1940–46.

## ❧ JONNY ON THE SPOT ❧

In 2001 Jonny Wilkinson amassed a record Six Nations Championship points tally with 89 (scoring one try, 24 conversions and 12 penalties).

## ❧ O'GARA'S RECORD-SETTING DAY ❧

On 5 February 2012, Ronan O'Gara joined Brian O'Driscoll as Ireland's most capped player. He came on as a substitute for Jonathan Sexton in the 76th minute of Ireland's 23–20 RBS Six Nations Championship defeat against Wales in Dublin. It was his 117th cap for his country. The game was also O'Gara's 57th appearance in the tournament, passing compatriot Mike Gibson's 56 games in the Five Nations between 1964–79. Three weeks later, O'Gara, Ireland's all-time leader in points scored and fifth in the world, passed O'Driscoll – who was injured for the 2012 Six Nations Championship – but still remained behind the centre in all-time international appearances. This is because O'Driscoll has represented the British & Irish Lions on four occasions more than O'Gara.

## ❧ SCOTT FOR THE SCOTS ❧

Matt Scott made his full international debut for Scotland in their 32–14 defeat against Ireland in the RBS Six Nations Championship in Dublin on 10 March 2012. He was the tenth player with the surname Scott to wear the thistle, and there have been a further six men with the first (or given) name Scott.

## ❧ LEIGH LEADS THE WAY ❧

Leigh Halfpenny of Grand Slam winners Wales was the leading points-scorer of the 2012 RBS Six Nations Championship with 66. Ireland's Tommy Bowe was the top try-scorer with five.

***Did You Know That?***
Bowe spent four seasons, 2008–12, playing club/provincial rugby in Wales for the Ospreys.

## ❧ PAYING THE ULTIMATE PRICE ❧

No fewer than 130 rugby international players lost their lives during World War 1. Of those, 26 had represented England, including the captain of their 1914 Grand Slam team, Ronald Poulton.

## 🎗 ITALY'S NEW LEADER 🎗

Following the 2011 IRB Rugby World Cup, Italy's coach Nick Mallett left the *Azzurri* to return to his Cape Town home and Frenchman Jacques Brunel replaced him. In 2001, then French national coach Bernard Laporte appointed Brunel to the technical staff, training the forwards. Brunel remained in the post until the 2007 Rugby World Cup.

*Did You Know That?*
Brunel coached Perpignan to the French National Championship in season 2008–09.

## 🎗 QUICK OFF THE MARK 🎗

Scotland's John Leslie holds the record for scoring the fastest try in international rugby. On 6 February 1999, playing for Scotland against Wales at Murrayfield, Leslie touched down just 10 seconds after the kick-off. It was the perfect start for the Scots in their opening game of the final Five Nations Championship before the arrival of Italy. They went on to win this match 33–20, and finished the competition as the last ever Five Nations champions.

## 🎗 SIX TOGETHER 🎗

In 2010, "Six Together" became the new official anthem for the RBS Six Nations Championship. The rousing theme tune was penned by The Howling Wolf Group, who consulted with Six Nations Rugby Limited over a two-year period. The main idea behind the tune was to encapsulate the sound from the various musical instruments and musical sounds for which each nation is famous: England gave a boy's cathedral choir; France provided an accordion; there are uilleann pipes for Ireland; the mandolin for Italy; Scotland naturally offered the unique sound of bagpipes; and from Wales came the sound of the Celtic harp.

## 🎗 WALES'S YOUNGEST EVER DRAGON 🎗

On 20 March 2010, Ospreys winger Tom Prydie became the youngest player ever to play an international for Wales. At the age of 18 years and 25 days, Prydie helped Wales to defeat Italy 33–10 at the Millennium Stadium, Cardiff, and ensured his country didn't finish bottom of the 2010 RBS Six Nations Championship table.

## ⚔ STILL UNBEATEN ⚔

After their victory over Ireland in 2013, England is now the only country that Italy has yet to beat in the Six Nations Championship.

## ⚔ A BORING SIX NATIONS ⚔

The 2013 RBS Six Nations Championship set new records for the fewest points, 534, and the fewest tries, 37.

## ⚔ STRANGELY DRAWN TO EACH OTHER ⚔

Louis Picamole's try and Frédéric Michalak's conversion in the last few minutes of France's 13–13 draw with Ireland at Aviva Stadium, Dublin, on 9 March 2013 meant that, for the second consecutive year, France and Ireland had played to a Six Nations Championship draw, this after the 17–17 deadlock in 2012. Not since England and Scotland had drawn in 1982 and 1983 had two countries finished all-square in consecutive years. It was only the fifth draw since Italy entered the competition in 2000 – in 210 matches – and the 66th since the Home Nations Championship began in 1883.

## ⚔ *AZZURRI* ON THE UP ⚔

In their final game of the 2013 RBS Six Nations Championship, Italy defeated Ireland 22–15 at Rome's Stadio Olimpico to give the *Azzurri* their first ever Six Nations victory over the Irish, and first since a 37–22 triumph in Bologna on 20 December 1997. Having already beaten France 23–18 in Rome in their opening fixture of 2013, it marked Italy's first two-win Six Nations since 2007.

## ⚔ SCREEN STARS ⚔

Ireland's dramatic final game of the 2009 RBS Six Nations Championship, when they defeated Wales at the Millennium Stadium, Cardiff, had a television audience of 945,000. The match was Ireland's most-watched TV programme all year.

## ⚔ NO CHANGE FOR HALFPENNY ⚔

Just as in 2012, Leigh Halfpenny finished the 2013 Six Nations Championship as the competition's leading scorer. He amassed 74 points from one try, six conversions and 19 penalties.

## 𝕄 POINTING AT THE POSTS 𝕄

When Wales defeated Scotland 28–18 at Murrayfield on 9 March 2013, the two teams set a new international rugby record with 18 penalty kick attempts. Greig Laidlaw amassed all 18 of Scotland's points with six successes in eight attempts, but he was overshadowed by Leigh Halfpenny. He netted 23 points from seven penalties and a successful conversion of the game's only try, by Richard Hibbard.

*Did You Know That?*
Wales set another record in the match: they achieved their Six Nations Championship best ever fifth consecutive away victory.

## 𝕄 A CAUSE FOR CELEBRATION 𝕄

Italy have celebrated victory in the Six Nations Championship only 11 times in 14 seasons, and never more than twice in one season.

| Year | Opponent | Venue | Score |
|------|----------|-------|-------|
| 2001 | Scotland | Rome | 34–20 |
| 2003 | Wales | Rome | 30–22 |
| 2004 | Scotland | Rome | 20–14 |
| 2007 | Scotland | Edinburgh | 37–17 |
| 2007 | Wales | Rome | 23–20 |
| 2008 | Scotland | Rome | 23–20 |
| 2010 | Scotland | Rome | 16–12 |
| 2011 | France | Rome | 22–21 |
| 2012 | Scotland | Rome | 13–6 |
| 2013 | France | Rome | 23–18 |
| 2013 | Ireland | Rome | 22–15 |

*Did You Know That?*
Scotland's 34–10 defeat of Italy decided who finished third in the 2013 Six Nations Championship. The points difference between them was 27, so a ten-point loss would have left Italy in a best-ever third.

## 𝕄 A BAD VINTAGE 𝕄

In the final year of the Five Nations Championship, 1999, France and Ireland shared the ignominy of the wooden spoon. History repeated itself in 2013 when both countries finished on three points, but France were officially placed last as their points difference was nine worse than the Irish.

# 𝒪
## ❧ INDEX ❧